MW01232112

GET IT RIGHT!

THE FIVE MOST IMPORTANT PLANNING CONCEPTS DOCTORS GET WRONG

JASON DYKEN, MD, MBA

Get It Right!

Jason Dyken
251-955-2827

DykenWealthStrategies.com

234 Office Park Dr.
Gulf Shores, AL 36542

ISBN-10: 1-946203-04-1
ISBN-13: 978-1-946203-04-5

—Disclaimer—

Paperback
Expert

www.PaperbackExpert.com

Table of Contents

Preface

Physicians in our society are the best and the brightest. The path of becoming a doctor is long, includes hard work, and requires many sacrifices. Despite these costs, doctors make sacrifices to become true professionals and take on the awesome responsibility of patient care. Aiming their every effort toward the care of others, doctors strive to become trusted advocates and help people through challenging times. They continually focus on the best possible treatment and outcome for the patient.

These reasons formed my motivation for entering the healthcare field. I studied through and graduated medical school, then practiced internal medicine for ten years. As a practitioner, I understand your burdens and commitments. Medicine is not merely a job: it is a real calling. And it's a calling you take very seriously.

I was raised in a family of health care providers. My father is a doctor, as is my uncle. My mother is a nurse. My sister has a doctoral degree, and a cadre of cousins is also in healthcare. My wife is an orthodontist—we met during medical school. My whole life has been spent around the healthcare industry; it's all I have ever really known. Business contacts, social interactions, friends and family—each revolves around individuals in this field.

Some might find that sad. Shouldn't I expand my horizons?

I don't think so. I love the healthcare profession, and I love those who dedicate their lives to it. As I interact with more professionals my respect only grows for their moral ethics, compassion, drive, and intellect. Society expects great things from its doctors; thus, healthcare professionals possess both an exceptional honor and a huge challenge.

Unfortunately, all too frequently doctors expend so much effort caring for patients, they have none left over for themselves and their families. Healthcare is challenging partly because it is all-encompassing. Medicine and dentistry can easily consume a doctor's life.

So what does this have to do with financial planning? Simply this: If you are to stay focused on your commitment to patient care, you must ensure your affairs are in order. You need to know your family is secure. How can you focus on and excel in your work with an unstable personal life and messy financial affairs? Diligently maintaining your focus is critical, and disordered affairs may cause a feeling of nagging guilt or all-out threat. Stability in your personal financial affairs can help free you to shine in your practice.

Doctors find ways to neglect themselves in the midst of their commitment to their patients. And if they do work with a financial advisor, the advice is often subpar (to say the least). During my ten years of active medical practice and fifteen years of financial advising, I have gathered a lot of insight into the world of personal finance. Hearing such poor financial advice directed toward doctors—or receiving it firsthand—continually shocks me.

Twenty-five years ago, a young married couple began planning their financial lives. As successful doctors, they understood their need for sound financial advice. So they interviewed various financial professionals. There were plenty to interview, for there is no shortage of people desiring to sell products to doctors (as you very well know).

This couple spoke to accountants, lawyers, investment managers, insurance agents, and more. Sometimes the advice they received was spot on. Other times it was downright criminal. One tax planning attorney asked if they wanted to cheat—they politely declined and announced that they must be going. Some accountants responded to tax planning questions by declaring, "You should be happy to pay taxes, because they represent economic success." Not exactly the answer this couple was looking for.

This couple slowly began to realize that no one shared their perspective on what financial planning should accomplish. No one seemed to understand their aims and financial goals. All these people focused on their specialty, their pet product, while ignoring the wider picture. They may have been really good at their niche, but they were unable to explain how their unique product impacted the overall plan. Focusing on providing the right solution had been replaced by focusing on product sales. Regardless of whether the product actually made sense for this young couple, the salesperson would force it into the shape of a "perfect solution." It was a continual game of fitting square pegs into round holes.

Moreover, the planners expressed no desire to consider the big picture. They had no interest in developing a successful holistic strategy in order to create the financial life this couple desired. They were consumed—not by client care, but by product sales and self-promotion. A comprehensive perspective was altogether absent.

This young couple was none other than my wife and myself. As an internist, I knew that beneficial patient outcomes depend on recognizing all the dynamics in play. Whether those factors are social, emotional, economic, or medical, they all impact the patient's health. Sometimes the difference between a patient living or dying rests on understanding the disease's broad context. This works in medicine, and I as a young practitioner I believed it would work in financial planning.

The broad context of goals for your financial life should drive your planning decisions. Yet the marketplace lacked any offer of assistance with this holistic effort. So, through trial and error (and some tribulation), I ended up planning my and my wife's own financial life. Later on I became involved with a planning organization that only worked with doctors. Additionally, I gained a few financial planning clients of my own. Finally, in 2001 I left the practice of medicine and committed myself full-time to working on doctors' financial planning needs. Now I run a "doctors only" firm, dedicated solely to helping doctors like you make sound monetary decisions.

Throughout my journey I've learned a lot. The financial services industry is complex, perhaps as confusing as the healthcare industry. Having an advocate to guide you can be of great benefit. I wrote this book in order to share a few insights, hopefully enabling you to navigate the treacherous waters of financial planning. These insights are contained within five main concepts, concepts I believe are essential to the financial success of all healthcare professionals. Unfortunately, many doctors misunderstand or misapply these core concepts, thereby pivoting toward financial disaster. All five concepts in combination form the basis of a successful financial plan.

In this book I will briefly overview the five concepts doctors get wrong, then delve further into each one. My goal is to aid you in recognizing the planning components and clearly perceiving how they fit together.

This book does not have enough space for me to share every necessary detail. However, I do want to give you compelling reasons to care about your financial life, as well as start you on the journey of change. You can maximum your income, minimize your taxes, and transition confidently from work to retirement. You can develop a comprehensive plan leading to security for your family. You can create a legacy of your life's work. Educate yourself on the five concepts in this book and you are well on your way.

I passionately desire that you get the best and most comprehensive understanding available. I want you to make truly informed decisions. Our goal is to help you reach the point of confidence—confidence that your finances are well positioned and that your future is secure—so that you will be free from stress and worry. You can return to focusing on your patients, return to the whole reason you first became a doctor: helping people.

You can get it right!

The Five Concepts

Doctors commonly get five concepts wrong. These are:

❶ Tax impact

❷ Beating the market

❸ Asset protection

❹ Holistic planning

❺ Asset conversion

You'll find a brief overview of these five concepts immediately below. In the following chapters, we will delve into each in turn.

1. Ignoring the impact of taxes

Most healthcare professionals do not understand that taxation will be the largest single expense of their lives. Because of this, they ignore the impact of taxes on their current lifestyle and future retirement.

I can predict this with little doubt: you **will** pay more for taxes than for your education, for your home, or for setting up your practice.

The Beatles understood this concept in their song "Taxman":

(if you drive a car, car;) – I'll tax the street;
(if you try to sit, sit;) – I'll tax your seat;
(if you get too cold, cold;) – I'll tax the heat;
(if you take a walk, walk;) – I'll tax your feet.

Don't ask me what I want it for
If you don't want to pay some more
Cause I'm the taxman,
Yeah, I'm the taxman.
— The Beatles

Acknowledging that the taxes you pay form your greatest lifetime expense is the first step. Now what can you do about it? If you can minimize these taxes by proactively addressing your tax burden, that should be an integral part of planning for your future. Thus, keeping your hard-earned dollars working for you (instead of Uncle Sam) is the first concept I will present.

Justice Learned Hand described the dual sides of our tax system in a famous quote:

"In America, there are two tax systems: one for the informed and one for the uninformed. Both are legal."

– Learned Hand

I aim to turn you into an informed taxpayer. In chapters to come we will look at a framework that will help you recognize the impact of taxes and understand your investment options. We'll consider three different types of investment accounts, including their current and future tax implications. These three tax "buckets" are the **Tax Deferred Bucket,** the **Taxable Bucket,** and the **Tax Advantaged Bucket.** Each operates differently, and within them you have the further decision of picking specific investments. Fully grasping the rightful place of these three buckets will substantially affect your planning.

During your working years, your goal is to allocate your invested dollars to take advantage of each bucket's unique benefits. Claiming these benefits will move you from the Uninformed Person Tax System to the Informed Person Tax System. And we all want to be in that second system, do we not?

You can be an informed taxpayer. You really can make effective investment decisions and help minimize the impact of taxes on your results.

2. Trying to beat the market

The second concept physicians and dentists commonly get wrong is beating the market. What's their mistake? That they even try.

Here's the truth: Investing your money with the purpose of beating the market is a loser's game. Despite the eternal media production revealing all these incredible market-beating secrets, reality is quite different. All the objective data shows that, over time, trying to pick individual stocks and time the market is a loser's game. (And do you really think the major broadcast networks give great investment advice?)

Successfully managing your investments to maximize market returns requires that you grasp a few major concepts. In the chapter on trying to beat the market, I will lay out investment best practices and identify key focus points in order to help minimize loss and capture gains. Plus, you will learn (perhaps for the first time) how to develop an investment strategy that is designed to help achieve your financial goals.

3. Leaving assets unprotected

The third financial planning concept doctors get wrong is asset protection. They do not understand the assets they possess, nor know the nuances of securing them—thus they leave assets unprotected.

Doctors face a lot of liability issues. You will find it advantageous to learn about each of these risks and their potential to undermine any (and all) of your planning. Developing a plan to diminish risk and protect your assets is essential. Ignoring the liability risks you face could result in the loss of your practice and personal wealth.

I could share many examples of doctors who suffered great loss due to an unexpected liability claim. Continuing to have both personal exposure and practice exposure opens you up to potential losses. These losses could take a huge bite out of your wealth, even subsequently preventing you from creating your financial life plan. Thorough and appropriate asset protection is vitally important.

In the chapter on asset protection we will look at your potential assets and liabilities. Then we will explore how to help secure those assets while diminishing the liabilities. You will see how your decisions for these first three planning concepts are interconnected, and will serve as the foundation of your retirement wealth.

4. Missing the big picture

The fourth concept is both the most important and the most overlooked. Holistic planning is where everything comes together. The concept is easy: You need to coordinate all the individual aspects of your retirement thinking into a well-oiled, coordinated, functional plan. Crossing many areas of expertise, such a plan requires a competent financial advisor who can operate in multiple realms.

Unfortunately, often the implementation of this easily understood concept fails. I talk to many doctors who claim they have a "guy," a great financial planner. But as we discuss in more detail, I find that they only have a product salesperson. The doctors have no idea what their plan is, what their goals are, and what achieving those goals will require. They have missed the big picture due to incomplete advice.

Even something as basic as the total dollar value of assets that will need to be saved to become financially independent is not addressed during a doctor's shortened saving window. What is your number? If you do not know, then you might be suffering from fragmented advice from a product salesperson—not a planner. Primarily because of this gaping hole in financial services for doctors, I have spent the last 15 years focused on helping doctors plan their future.

In concept 4 we will consider the economic life cycle, so you can identify where you are in your planning life. Once you know your location, you will know the type of planning you need.

Then I will present a framework describing the four main cornerstones of planning. We implement this comprehensive plan using our proprietary C.U.R.E. process.

5. Converting assets to income inefficiently

At last, you have navigated the first four concepts and are nearing retirement. How do you convert your investment savings into a tax-efficient income stream lasting your entire life?

The fifth concept doctors get wrong is asset conversion. They fail to plan for the conversion of hard-earned assets into a spendable income source. Doctors are well versed in investing, and there is no shortage of willing advisors to take on your money management needs. The focus is on accumulating assets.

So let's say that you have successfully navigated this aspect of your financial path. Now what? How do you convert these assets into income? That is the only way you can stop working for income. Everyone wants to help you save and invest your money, but seldom do I encounter anyone with a well-structured plan to convert assets into income.

How do you actually generate money to buy groceries and go visit the grandkids? Moreover, how do you do so in a tax-efficient manner? Creating an income plan requires a specific skill set. This income plan is more than generating a dividends check every quarter. It includes identifying all your sources of income and assessing the tax implications. In a future chapter, I will sketch out a five-step formulation that will help you most efficiently convert your assets to income.

The key word is "efficiently." Anyone can convert assets to income—albeit with a huge chunk gone to Uncle Sam. Converting assets efficiently so you get as much income as possible is crucial.

Putting it all together

These are the five concepts where doctors tend to miss the mark. If you dig down to thoroughly understand these concepts and the options within each, you can emerge with a solid financial plan.

Doctors are in a great profession for job security: They'll always have patients because people will always get sick. Not many businesses have guaranteed customers! When run correctly, a healthy practice has no shortage of patients. Couple the endless stream of patients with a solid reimbursement model, and you have the ability to create the financial life of your dreams.

Over the last 25 years of working with doctors—10 of those as a fellow practitioner and 15 as a planner—I have seen the good, the bad, and the ugly of financial planning. I've witnessed doctors fail to attain their goals. I've known doctors who were never able to retire. I've sat with doctors through incredible financial chaos and confusion.

Your financial life does not have to experience these hardships. Success is not a matter of chance. In the following pages, we will dive deeper into these five concepts. You will grow in your understanding of how to avoid these common mistakes.

If implemented correctly, the five financial planning concepts in this book will help you reach your financial goals. They will help you get on the rigth road to financial independence, monetary freedom, and the ability to leave a legacy of your life's work.

Concept #1.

Ignoring the Impact of Taxes

Three tax buckets

The first concept of financial life planning so many physicians and dentists misunderstand is the impact of taxes on their wealth accumulation for their future.

You know you pay a lot in taxes. You shell out for income tax, property tax, sales tax, business license taxes, gas tax, corporate taxes, and on and on and on. Getting a handle on this issue is incredibly important!

Here is another great quote from Justice Learned Hand about our tax system:

Over and over again courts have said that there is nothing sinister in so arranging one's affairs as to keep taxes as low as possible. Everybody does so, rich or poor; and all do right, for nobody owes any public duty to pay more than the law demands: taxes are enforced exactions, not voluntary contributions. To demand more in the name of morals is mere cant.
Commissioner v. Newman, 159 F2d 848 (1947).[1]

---

1 https://scholar.google.com/scholar_case?case=6284821606579578514

The law defines the taxes that we are required to pay. Understanding the law and your opportunities to minimize the tax burden is your choice. Our complicated tax code has been written to afford certain privileges to informed taxpayers. These options are legal, and very much incentivized by our political system and the leaders who established the tax code.

We should always give to Caesar what belongs to Caesar, but anything above the amount required by law is a voluntary contribution. Would you rather donate to your favorite charity or to the government? If you believe politicians know best when it comes to spending your money, then by all means keep paying both your legal obligation and your voluntary contribution. If not, then continue to read. We will frame how best to evaluate your options and give you ideas on how to restructure your planning for success.

You have options in dealing with taxes—particularly, you can make three distinct investment choices. Perhaps it will be helpful to refer to these three choices as "buckets." The three tax buckets are:

○ Bucket Number 1 – Tax Deferred Bucket

○ Bucket Number 2 – Taxable Bucket

○ Bucket Number 3 – Tax Advantaged Bucket

Look at the diagram below. It's a simple sketch of the basic taxation scenarios that exist when it comes to your salary, your assets, and creating your future retirement wealth.

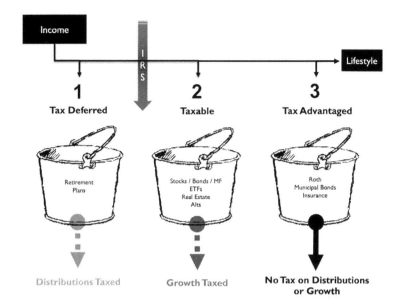

See the box in the upper left-hand corner with the arrow moving to the right? This represents your income pipeline—the money you make as a practicing doctor. You make money, you pay your employees, you pay your business expenses, and hopefully some money is left over. That leftover money presents you with the first choice in your personal financial planning. You can take that money as salary, or you can invest it into a pre-tax savings vehicle.

The Tax Deferred bucket

Enter the **Tax Deferred bucket.** Most retirement planning platforms fall into this bucket. Retirement investments are often referred to as "qualified plans," "pension plans," or "retirement plans." These tax-deferred investment options allow you to save money before the IRS takes its share. You can put away your earnings before taxes and watch them grow before the tax bite.

Moreover, the assets in the bucket have the potential to increase without ongoing taxation. That is, not only the original contributions but also the ongoing growth are tax-deferred. This is what we call tax-deferred growth.

So two benefits that might lead a person to choose the tax-deferred bucket are pre-tax savings and tax-deferred growth. Let's consider an example to clarify matters.

Your two choices

	Option 1: Taxable	Option 2: Tax Deferred
Gross Income	$ 500,000	$ 500,000
minus Tax Deferred Contribution	$ -	$ 54,000
equals **Taxable Income**	$ 500,000	$ 446,000
minus 40% Tax	$ (200,000)	$ (178,400)
equals **Net Income**	$ 300,000	$ 267,600
minus Taxable Contribution	$ 54,000	
equals **Spendable Income**	$ 246,000	$ 267,600
Totals		
Total Contribution	54,000	54,000
Total Tax Paid	$ (200,000)	$ (178,400)

Take a look at Option 1. This hypothetical example assumes that you make $500,000 of gross income this year. You decide not to make any tax-deferred contributions. When the tax man comes knocking, you must pay taxes on the full amount.

Since most doctors are in the top tax bracket, the example also assumes a 40% income tax for easy math. So, with $500,000 of salary, you owe the IRS 40%, or $200,000. Now you have $300,000 left over.

You decide to take $54,000 from that $300,000 and invest it. That gives you $246,000 to live on. You can use this money to fund your lifestyle, as well as save for the future.

Tracking so far? Now let's compare that with Option 2.

In Option 2, you have the same $500,000 income. But before Uncle Sam demands his portion, you sock $54,000 away in a tax-deferred retirement vehicle. In other words, you employ the Tax Deferred Bucket.

That $54,000 tax-deferred investment has the potential to grow without incurring any ongoing taxes. You do not pay taxes on the growth of your money when it is invested in a 401k, an IRA, or another tax-deferred investment vehicle.

Because you put $54,000 into that retirement vehicle **before** taxes, your total taxable income is now only $446,000. You are still taxed at 40%, but 40% of $446,000 is just $178,400. That tax bill is $21,600 less than in Option 1! Additionally, you have $267,600 left to pay for your lifestyle expenses.

Have you followed this illustration? Make sure you understand it before moving on. Go back and look at the graphic if you need to. The key difference is where you decide to put the $54,000 in savings: the Taxable bucket, or the Tax Deferred bucket. That decision affects your tax burden both today and later.

Two choices and the future

To summarize, when you get your paycheck you have a choice. You can choose to take all the money as salary and put it toward mortgage payments, back-to-school clothes, peanut butter, and birthday presents. Or you can decide to put some of your money into a tax-deferred plan.

Fewer initial taxes and untaxed growth are great benefits. However, a downside does exist. Suppose your $54,000 tax-deferred investment grows until it becomes $200,000. Hooray! You are now $146,000 richer. But are you really?

See, no tax is due while this $200,000 is tucked away in your retirement plan. But look back at the Three Buckets graphic, and notice the arrow coming out of the Tax Deferred bucket. That arrow represents the distribution of money from your tax-deferred investments which will be taxed at whatever the tax rate is at the time the funds are distributed.

The IRS wants a chunk of any money you move through that arrow. As soon as you withdraw money from the Tax Deferred bucket, you must pay income taxes on it. And you must pay taxes on the full amount, not merely the initial investment. In our example, you would be taxed on the $200,000 that comes out of the bucket, instead of the $54,000 that went in. At a 40% tax rate, your savings of $21,600 in Year One has turned into a back-end tax bill of $80,000 years later. Compound this scenario throughout years of plan contributions, and you can imagine that the numbers grow enormous.

Would you rather pay tax on the $54,000 seed or the $200,000 harvest? As you see, deferral makes you pay a price.

Conventional wisdom states that tax deferral is a good choice, despite the increased tax burden. Many individuals believe they will be in a lower tax bracket in the future. This is likely true for much of the population, but I believe it is most likely improbable for most doctors. Adopting the assumptions of this conventional wisdom may devastate your retirement. You must consider your individual reality.

What do you think will happen to tax rates in the future? The U.S. National Debt is currently over $19 trillion. How will we overcome this problem as a country? Many doctors believe, and I concur, that **future tax rates will increase.** This raises the stakes on Tax Deferred money. If rates go up, even more tax could be due on your deferred accounts during retirement—unless you strategize appropriately.

When you invest in a tax deferred retirement plan, you do receive tax benefits on the front end. You can take a practice deduction. It reduces personal taxable income. However, the disadvantage is that you create a future tax liability. And that liability may come due at a higher tax rate than you would have paid **if you had taken your money as salary earlier.** That is the challenge: trying to predict the future. Nonetheless, the Tax Deferred bucket can be a useful option as you plan your financial future.

Taxable bucket

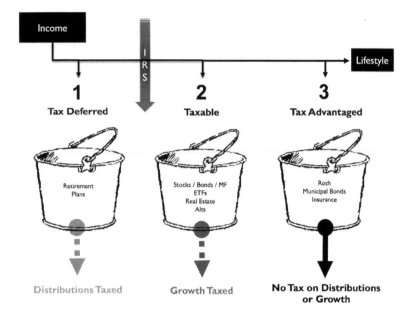

Take another look at the Three Buckets illustration. To the right of the IRS line, you see two buckets into which you can place post-tax earnings. You take your salary, you pay your income taxes, and now you can invest what you have remaining after lifestyle expenses. Your investment options are the Taxable bucket (the biggest bucket that most people choose) and the Tax Advantaged bucket.

Inside the **Taxable bucket** reside all kinds of post-tax investment accounts:

○ Stocks

○ Bonds

○ Mutual funds

- Exchange traded funds
- Real estate
- Other alternatives

All those belong in the Taxable bucket. You already paid income tax on the capital that you invest in such vehicles. This tax basis will not be taxed in the future, because you already paid Uncle Sam before you invested. However, as your money grows inside the Taxable bucket, **all growth is taxed.** Unlike the Tax Deferred bucket (where growth is not taxed), all growth in the Taxable bucket is subject to tax. It leaks tax.

For example, say you have $100,000 in the Taxable bucket. If it grows to $120,000, you will pay tax on the $20,000 in growth. This would be either ordinary income tax (in case of a dividend payment) or a capital gains tax on appreciation when you liquidate the position. Remember: The original $100,000 you put in the Taxable bucket consists of post-tax dollars you will not need to pay tax on again. Only the growth is taxed.

Tax Advantaged bucket

As for the third bucket, most people do not participate in it—or even know about it. This is the **Tax Advantaged Bucket**. Like the Taxable bucket, this option is a post-tax investment. The IRS has already taken its cut. However, in this bucket **growth is not taxed.** Over time, this compounding of growth without ongoing taxation can create significant wealth.

Look at this example of tax deferred growth:

$100,000 Invested at 6% over 30 Years

	1	5	10	15	20	25	30
Invested tax deferred	$106,000	$133,823	$179,085	$239,656	$320,714	$429,187	$574,349
Invested with 20% tax	$104,800	$126,417	$159,813	$202,032	$255,403	$322,873	$408,168
Invested with 40% tax	$103,600	$119,344	$142,429	$169,979	$202,859	$242,099	$288,930

Invested tax deferred —— Invested with 20% tax —— Invested with 40% tax

This hypothetical example is used for comparison purposes and is not intended to represent the past or future performance of any investment. No withdrawals were made during the period indicated. Actual returns will fluctuate. Taxable account assumes earnings are taxed as ordinary income. Lower maximum rates on capital gains and dividends would make the taxable accounts returns more favorable when compared with the tax-deferred account. The types of securities and strategies illustrated may not be suitable for everyone. Some investments that are free of federal income taxes may be subject to state and local taxes. Also, the alternative minimum tax may apply. Fees and other expenses were not considered in the illustration. Withdrawals from a tax-deferred program are subject to ordinary income taxes. If a withdrawal is taken before age 59½, a 10% federal tax penalty may apply. Individuals should consider their time frame and income tax brackets when evaluating a financial instrument.

Source: http://www.ceterarepondemand.com/resource-center/investment/taxable-vs-tax-deferred-:

See how the tax-deferred investment grows the most? Obviously, untaxed growth will multiply more quickly than taxed growth. The key is that the Tax Advantaged bucket shares this advantage, minus the disadvantage! That distinction could mean the difference between missing and reaching your financial goals.

In both the Tax Deferred bucket (#1) and the Tax Advantaged bucket (#3) growth occurs without ongoing taxation. But here is where the Tax Advantaged bucket gets even more exciting.

Remember the downside to the Tax Deferred bucket? When you need the money, you must pay the tax man on the distribution. But the Tax Advantaged bucket is different—thus the name Tax **Advantaged**. It enables you to take money back out of this bucket without a taxable event occurring. In other words, you get **tax-free withdrawals.** Most people do not realize this. For the Tax Advantaged bucket, money goes in post-tax, grows tax-deferred, and is accessed tax-free. When you take money out of the bucket for your retirement lifestyle, you lose nothing to taxation.

The Tax Advantaged bucket is the opposite of the Tax Deferred bucket. Tax Deferred means no tax on the seed, but tax on the harvest. Tax Advantaged means tax on the seed, but no tax on the harvest.

As you plan for retirement, you will encounter choices concerning these three tax buckets. Each bucket has a distinct and significant impact on your tax burden and your disposable income. A touch of education and strategy can help minimize your tax liability and maximize your retirement wealth.

Three buckets, many options

Each bucket proffers many investment decision points. You need to decide what type of investment vehicle to employ within each bucket, based on how it will impact your tax situation. Once you understand the pros and cons, you can make a strategic decision as to which buckets to use, as well as how to place your funds within each bucket you choose.

Tax strategy #1 – Tax Deferred investment options

Many kinds of retirement plans offer tax deferral benefits. Some are "qualified" retirement plans, and others are not qualified plans but have similar characteristics. Here is a table showing five of your options, along with the maximum allowable contribution.

Tax Deferred Investment Options

Plan	Surplus Practice Income / Contribution
401k – Roth Optional	$18,000 ($24,000 if age 50)
401k w/ Profit Sharing	$54,000 ($60,000 if age 50)
Defined Benefit / Cash Balance Plan*	Above $54,000
	$180,000 for age 45
	$280,000 for age 55
Combination Plan 401k PS w/ DB*	$215,000 for age 45
	$320,000 for age 55
Captive Insurance Company	Surplus Income above $500,000

* These are approximate contribution examples. Results will vary due to income, age, maximum allowed, etc.

Source: https://retirenews.net/2016/10/27/irs-announces-retirement-plan-limits-for-2017/

This summary is designed to provide an overview of the dollar limitations for retirement plans applicable in 2017 and is not intended to be comprehensive. For a complete announcement of the applicable limits see IRS Notice 2016-62 and Social Security Administration's 2017 Social Security Changes Fact Sheet.

This summary is for general information only and is believed to be accurate and reliable as of posting date but may be subject to change. Not investment, tax, or legal advice. Individuals should seek services from the appropriate tax and legal professionals as to applicability of this information for their individual circumstances.

The first basic tax-deferred retirement plan is a simple **401K Roth** optional plan. This is first-stage investing, and you can defer up to $18,000 of your salary annually into this plan. Are you age 50 or above? Then you can take advantage of the catch-up provision and put $24,000 away per year. This is a nice savings plan for anyone to start with. Typically, these plans are coupled with a company match. Depending on how much surplus you have and how much your lifestyle costs are, you can invest $18,000 (or $24,000) plus company match into this bucket.

The second plan is a **401K with profit sharing**. The profit-sharing component allows you to contribute more into the plan for the plan participants. As of 2017, with the addition of a profit-sharing component you can put away up to $54,000. If you are age 50 or above, the maximum you can put away is $60,000. A few key factors influence that maximum amount:

the amount of surplus you want to add to this plan, and how complex a plan you want to employ. You can add more money through a combination of salary deferrals, safe harbor matching, and profit-sharing contributions.

Both of these 401Ks are called "defined contribution plans." That is, you are defining exactly how much money you want to put away. You are defining the contribution amount.

The third plan is **a defined benefit plan**, also called **a cash balance plan**. These operate quite differently from a defined contribution plan. In the defined benefit plan, you define your benefit—the amount of money you want to accumulate. Then you work backwards to calculate how much money you must contribute every year to reach that future benefit. This involves actuarial calculations, which depend on factors such as your age, the number of your employees, the demographics of your group, and how many other plan participants there are.

The defined benefit plan's maximum is typically higher than the defined contribution plan's $54,000 maximum. As a general estimate, if you are 45 then you can put away $180,000 per year into a defined benefit plan. If you are 55 then you can put away $280,000. Again, the numbers will be designed specifically for your unique circumstances. These are general guidelines. And as you can see, these defined benefit plans allow for significantly more contributions than the first two defined contribution plans.

I talk to many doctors who have only ever heard about the 401K. They say, "I can only put away $54,000." On the contrary—I have worked with many doctors who contribute well in excess of six figures each year. For this reason, educating yourself to understand the legally available options is important. Do you have the capacity to save more than $54,000 into a retirement plan? The defined benefit plan allows you to do so.

The ability to potentially invest over six figures per year pre-tax will radically change your wealth outlook. Remember the example I used earlier? Imagine taking a six-figure deduction from your salary every year! Plug in the numbers and see how much you can save in taxes. Additionally, that much money in a tax-deferred account can do wonders for reaching your savings goals. Caution is warranted, though—you are creating a future tax liability. Balance between the buckets is key.

To Defer or Not To Defer?

	Option 1: Taxable	Option 2: Tax Deferred	Option 3: Tax Deferred
Gross Income	$ 500,000	$ 500,000	$ 500,000
minus Tax Deferred Contribution	$ -	$ 54,000	$ 150,000
equals **Taxable Income**	$ 500,000	$ 446,000	$ 350,000
minus 40% Tax	$ (200,000)	$ (178,400)	$ (140,000)
equals **Net Income / Spendable**	$ 300,000	$ 267,600	$ 210,000
minus Taxable Contribution	$ 54,000	$ -	$ -
equals **Spendable Income**	$ 246,000	$ 267,600	$ 210,000
Totals			
Total Savings	54,000	54,000	150,000
Total Tax Paid	$ (200,000)	$ (178,400)	$ (140,000)

The fourth retirement plan is a **combination plan.** As the name implies, it combines both a defined contribution plan and a defined benefit plan. This can allow you to sock away even higher amounts than with either plan alone. For age 45, you can invest about $215,000; for age 55, about $320,000. These are general guidelines, not set caps on what you can put away. As with defined benefit plans, the final numbers are based on complex factors. Nonetheless, there are ways to defer tax and capture savings for just about any amount of practice-generated revenue. Time taken to evaluate your options is time well spent.

The fifth and final tax deferred savings plan is a **captive insurance company**. A captive insurance company is basically an insurance company that the doctor owns. Here's how it works.

Most doctors' practices have inherent risks. That is simply the nature of a healthcare practice. These risks include malpractice claims, insurance audits, and regulatory oversight. Sometimes you can purchase insurance to protect yourselves from these risks. Sometimes you cannot. A captive insurance company is basically a physician establishing and owning an insurance company, providing his practice with coverage for the risks they cannot get insurance for in the open marketplace. The healthcare practice pays premiums to the insurance company, in return receiving insurance against events that may or may not happen.

If the risk event occurs, the insurance policy covers the risk and the insurance company sends the healthcare practice a check. If nothing ever happens, the premium dollars go into the insurance company as reserves and profit. Since the doctor owns the insurance company, he also owns the company's profits. For your healthcare practice, the premiums are a deductible expense. Yet the premium money either return to the practice for a future liability or else became capital in a company the doctor owns. Ultimately, taking money out of the captive insurance company can have a positive net tax impact.

The captive insurance company is not a qualified retirement plan. However, from a tax standpoint it operates similarly to the other tax-deferred retirement plans. This is a very complicated vehicle, but it might be appropriate for doctors who need to capture funds exceeding $500,000 a year.

Every doctor is unique and every practice is unique. Appropriately utilizing the plans available in the Tax Deferred bucket requires insight, as well as a big picture viewpoint. Tailoring a plan to address the doctor's unique situation will derive the maximum benefit over the long term.

In summary, many tax-deferred options are available. A doctor can invest an amount from as low as $10,000 per year to well over $500,000 per year. In fact, it is almost impossible for a doctor to make more money than we can legally put away in tax-deferred savings to secure their financial future.

Over the past 25 years, I have worked with or talked to numerous doctors who do not even know these kinds of opportunities exist. They need to put away substantial sums, but they never knew they could. Because of this I am passionate to ensure doctors find solid and comprehensive information about their options.

Tax strategy #2 – Taxable investment options

This strategy deals with investment plans available in the second bucket, the Taxable bucket.

Recall that you have already paid taxes on this money. It went into your wages and you paid your marginal income tax rate to the IRS. Out of the remaining amount you paid the mortgage, purchased groceries, and took care of other expenses. Now you have some extra to invest.

Investing in the Taxable bucket offers you a wide range of options: stocks, bonds, mutual funds, exchange traded funds (ETFs), real estate, alternatives, and many others. This bucket is taxable, so any income you derive from these investments becomes part of your taxable income (or is taxed as capital gains). Taxes continually leak out of this bucket. But the Taxable bucket also provides you with a number of advantages. It is best to work with an experienced financial advisor to determine what is appropriate for your individual situation. The price you pay for this liquidity is the lack of tax benefits. However, in some situations you can obtain tax advantages. For instance, if you invest in real estate—either directly or as part of a non-traded real estate investment trust—you can access unique depreciation allowances. Depreciation might enable you to write off or offset the income you derive. In the end, your return on investment would be taxed at a rate less than the maximum.

Another opportunity in the taxable bucket option is a limited partnership in the oil and gas industry. Historically, our country's tax code has incentivized domestic oil and gas production as a matter of social policy. For this reason, some oil and gas ventures allow investors to receive tax credits for domestic production. These tax credits take the form of depreciation, depletion allowances, and intangible drilling costs. They operate to directly or indirectly offset income, thus decreasing your taxes. Your choice of investments within the Taxable bucket impacts your tax liability.

Note that investments in real estate or oil and gas are typically not as liquid as other taxable investment options. Compared to investments in the publicly traded markets, you are tied in for a longer period. Balancing investment choice, expected returns, liquidity needs, and tax benefits is important in all planning decisions.[2]

---

2 Investing in real estate and real estate investment trusts (REITs) involve special risk, such as, limited liquidity, changes in tax laws, tenant turnover or defaults, competition, casualty losses and use of leverage. Real estate values may fluctuate based on economic and other factors. An investment in real estate or REITs may not be suitable for all investors and there are no assurances that the investment objectives of any real estate program will be attained.

Limited partnerships are subject to special risks, such as illiquidity and those inherent in the underlying investments. There are no assurance that the stated investment objectives will be reached. At redemption, the partnership shares may be worth more or less than the original investment. Individuals must meet specific suitability standards and should read the prospectus carefully before investing.

Tax strategy #3 – Tax Advantaged investment options

This bucket is my personal favorite. It contains incredible wealth-creating opportunities. Why? Because in it you minimize your tax burden. Would you not prefer to keep your money and invest it in your future?

Money invested in the Tax Advantaged bucket grows tax-deferred, like the Tax Deferred bucket and unlike the Taxable bucket. But the Tax Advantaged bucket is different because money you remove from it is not taxed. No ongoing taxation on growth, and no taxation when you liquidate.

Roth IRAs are in this bucket. Here we must distinguish between the two types of Individual Retirement Accounts: Traditional and Roth. The traditional IRA is basically an individual retirement plan with the same characteristics as a 401K. You put money into the IRA as a pretax contribution. The funds have the potential to grow tax-deferred over time. When you need the funds, they are taxed just like other plans in the Tax Deferred bucket. So the traditional IRA is in bucket 1.

The Roth IRA is different: You put your money in after income taxes. The money grows in a tax deferred account (no taxes on earnings). When you withdraw funds, there is no tax on distribution or growth.

The only problem with the Roth IRAs is its income restrictions on participation. Most doctors make too much money to be qualified to contribute to a Roth IRA. I talk to many doctors who indicate they would invest in a Roth IRA if they could, but they cannot because their Adjusted Gross Income (AGI) is too high.

However, you may still be able to participate in a Roth IRA. You can either utilize a backdoor Roth IRA strategy or convert an existing IRA into a Roth IRA. How do these two strategies work?

In the backdoor Roth IRA strategy, you contribute to a **non-deductible IRA** on a yearly basis. At some point, you take this and convert it into a Roth IRA. Since the funds that established the account were not pretax funds (that's the "non-deductible" part), only the growth is taxable upon conversion. Once the conversion is made, all future growth and distributions from this account will be tax free.

Another way a doctor can participate in a Roth IRA is by converting an existing **traditional IRA** into a Roth IRA. As you recall, there are income limits for contributing to a Roth IRA, and most doctors are ineligible. However, the conversion of existing IRA accounts has no such restriction. When you convert, all the money in the account will be taxed as ordinary income in the year of the conversion. Basically, you are gaining future tax-free distributions in exchange for a tax bill today. This is a smart move if you believe future tax rates will be higher than those today.

Is there a way to decrease this conversion tax? One strategy is to make the conversion (or partial conversion) in a year you earned income lower than usual. Also, if you experience an investment loss—which I'm sure you never do—those losses may help diminish the conversion tax cost that year. As you can tell, the issue is complex. Evaluate all options, costs, and benefits before making a decision of this magnitude. Individuals should seek services from the appropriate tax and legal professionals as to applicability of this information for their individual circumstances.

Another Tax Advantaged bucket investment option is **individual municipal bonds**. If you purchase municipal bonds and hold them to maturity, the income on them is typically not taxable. You do not receive these benefits with municipal bond funds—only individual city issuances. You should also buy them in the state where you reside in order to get the full federal and state tax benefits.

Developing a laddered portfolio of individual municipal bonds with different maturities can create a stable tax-efficient income stream. However, bond rates have been suppressed since 2008, so getting reasonable returns may be problematic. Also, the income derived from municipal bonds can impact the calculations of future Social Security and Medicare benefit taxation. Again, as with any planning issue, this topic is more complex than one short paragraph. If you are interested in this strategy, please consult an expert in municipal bonds to ensure you can achieve your desired objectives within the parameters of your risk tolerance.

Finally, one of the most underutilized vehicles for tax-free growth and tax-free income is a properly designed **permanent life insurance policy.** These plans are used by many of the top Fortune 500 companies and the executives who work there. However, they have been underutilized by the medical community.

Please do not fast forward through this section. This is important! I realize doctors do not like insurance. They do not like talking about insurance. They must hassle insurance companies all day long to get compensation for their services. Understandably, insurance companies are not well-beloved by health care professionals.

But misunderstanding about insurance abounds. Moreover, not all insurance is created equal. The right policy and the right understanding can cause a tectonic shift in your finances. I'm speaking specifically about permanent life insurance, and even more descriptively, about a well-designed indexed universal life (IUL) policy.

Why do people buy life insurance in the first place? Two reasons. One is the **death benefit:** You want to be assured of a source of funds or a lump sum payment to your loved ones in the event of your death. You want to cover any debts you may have and provide income for your family.

Two different types of insurance provide a death benefit: term insurance and permanent insurance. Term insurance is like renting an apartment. You have a contract to receive a certain benefit, and when the contract expires the benefit is no longer available. If you die during the contract period, a death benefit will be paid to your beneficiaries. Term insurance is great for younger doctors who are trying to protect their family's future, provide future income, and cover their family's needs.

Permanent life insurance is like term insurance in that part of the premium goes toward the death benefit. The other part of the premium, however, goes into an account that accrues value and builds equity for you. This is like buying a home instead of renting an apartment. With a home, part of the mortgage payment goes toward the interest, and some of it goes toward the principal. The principal reduction amount adds value to your home. In the same way, account values in an insurance policy can grow and provide you with unique benefits.

Different types of permanent insurance exist. These qualify as tax-deferred vehicles and can be separated into different types based on how they credit and accumulate funds. The three main types are:

- Whole Life

- Variable Life

- Indexed Universal Life

In whole life policies, the portion of your premiums not used for the death benefit is invested with the general accounts of the insurance company, typically in long-term bond positions. These are conservative investments which generate conservative returns consistent with fixed-income investments.

On the other end of the risk spectrum are variable life policies. In variable life, you own investments directly in the stock and bond markets and generate returns that these markets provide. This is riskier than investing in a whole life policy.

In between these two policies lie indexed universal life policies. With IUL, you receive returns credited to the cash value account based on a defined market index. The money is not invested in the market—just credited consistent with the returns generated by the market index. The money is part of the general ledger of the insurance company (just like an investment in whole life) but is credited in a manner that provides higher potential upside returns. This IUL policy is another viable option in the Tax Advantaged bucket. Cash value within an IUL policy grows tax-deferred, and the account value can be accessed tax-free.

This illustrates the other reason you buy life insurance. It is for the **living benefit:** that is, accessing the death benefit while you're alive. The living benefit is what makes IUL a valuable part of the Tax Advantaged bucket, because it allows you to use permanent life insurance as an investible asset. This asset can grow and create sustained tax free benefits for the future. A future chapter will share more about the crediting strategy and the development of living benefits in IUL.

These are the major options in the Tax Advantaged Bucket: Roth IRAs, municipal bonds, and permanent life insurance.

○ Roth IRAs have some complex rules and restrictions which may limit their use.

○ Municipal bonds are limited because you can only obtain the full tax benefit from issuances from your state of residence. Additionally, today's interest rates are less than attractive.

○ Properly designed IUL policies have less restrictions than Roth IRAs and have crediting rates that can be substantially higher than municipal bonds. There are higher contribution rates available and more flexibility in access to your funds. I personally choose this strategy to maximize the Tax Advantaged bucket.

The disadvantage to these vehicles is that they typically have a long-term investment horizon of five, ten, or even more years. This is not to say you cannot access any of your value before that time—you can. Unfortunately, there are penalties and costs associated with this early access.

As we consider the Three Buckets illustration a final time, you can see the wide range of choices available when planning your financial future. The buckets you choose to invest in will have varying implications for your current and future tax liabilities. And within each bucket, there are further current and future tax implications.

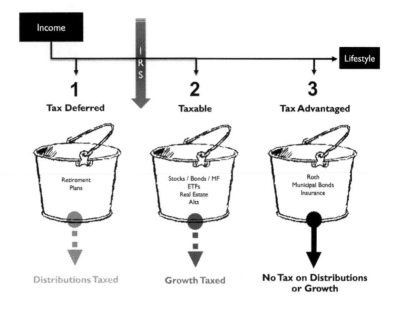

1	2	3
Tax Deferred	**Taxable**	**Tax Advantaged**
Retirement Plans	Stocks / Bonds / MF ETFs Real Estate Alts	Roth Municipal Bonds Insurance
Distributions Taxed	Growth Taxed	**No Tax on Distributions or Growth**

All this complexity does have an upside: you can minimize taxes and maximize your income. That is everyone's goal, and rightly so. As Justice Learned Hand once stated:

"Any one may so arrange his affairs that his taxes shall be as low as possible; he is not bound to choose that pattern which will best pay the Treasury; there is not even a patriotic duty to increase one's taxes."

Helvering v. Gregory, 69 F.2d 809, 810-11 (2d Cir. 1934)

You want to structure your investments to maximally support your professional and personal needs, wants, and wishes. Being savvy about your tax burden and investible dollars is the first step toward financial freedom and independence.

Concept #2.

Trying to Beat the Market

The second most important financial planning concept doctors get wrong pertains to investment management. Many doctors have the mindset of "beating the market" to reach their financial goals.

What does it mean to try to beat the market? And what is the market? The market is the public exchange established to sell shares in stocks, bonds, and other financial instruments. The market is established to link buyers and sellers together so they can exchange these instruments in an open and public way.

When I use the term "the markets," I am referring to the entire scope of the publicly traded establishment. Specifically, it refers to all the stocks and bonds within the public sector. Market returns are the growth in the holdings of the entire universe of publicly traded vehicles.

You can divide the public market into general categories, such as equities (stock) and fixed income (bonds). Each of these categories can be subdivided into asset classes: small cap, large value, small value, and many more. Each asset class can then be further broken down into smaller groupings. It is like one big file cabinet with folders and subfolders.

When you look at the "market" you need to know what part of the markets you are referencing. There are also established 'indexes' that combine a group of holdings to represent different parts of the market.

The Dow Jones Industrial average is a price-weighted average of 30 significant stocks traded on the NYSE. When the TV networks say "the market is up today" they are generally referring to the Dow.

The Standard & Poor 500 Index is another measure of the market. It contains 500 of the largest stocks in the US, making it a tool to gauge the overall health of large American companies.

In common vernacular, beating the market is getting better returns on your own accounts than the standardized and publicized average returns of the market at large (as represented by specific indices). In short, it's getting a return on your investment better than the overall market's return. *Indices are unmanaged and their returns assume reinvestment of dividends and do not reflect any fees or expenses. Investors cannot invest directly in an index.*

To delve into why trying to "beat the market" is a flawed investment strategy, let's unpack two basic investing principles.

The first is to **minimize your loss in a down market.**

The second is to **differentiate active and passive investing.**

You can act to minimize the negative impact of a bear market, and you can choose an investment style to suit your goals. Both these principles are far more important than beating the market.

Investment principle #1 – Minimize loss

All individuals want to minimize loss in their portfolios. Obviously, everyone wants to win and not to lose. But how can you ensure gain, or at least ensure minimal loss? Let's step back and take a wider look at what the markets are and which direction the markets are heading.

What are the markets? For the purposes of this discussion, when I talk about the markets, I'm referring to the broad concept of **growth in the value of companies in the public markets.** These capital markets are the representation and manifestation of the concept of capitalism. A company produces a good or service, sells it, and makes a profit. The owners of the company share these profits amongst themselves, while customers receive the good or service. Good companies grow and expand. Bad companies waste their resources and fail. The markets "keep score" of the winners and losers. The direction of the markets represents the success or failure of these companies.

Which direction are the markets heading? Over a short time-frame, the true answer is, "Nobody really knows." Prognostication and prediction abounds, but historically, high rates of accuracy over the short term are rare. However, the long term is somewhat easier to predict.

Consider the S&P 500, which is a good measure of the U.S. economy's overall health. If you listen to all the hype and headlines surrounding the financial markets over the last 10 years, you know we've had a pretty rough ride. People have called it "the lost decade." Out of the last 10 years (from 2006 to 2015), how many do you think were negative? How about the last 30 years?

The S&P over the Last 30 Years

Result	Year	Date	Rate of Return	Average Annual Rate of Return
90% Up Only down 1 year: *1990–91 Recession* Iraq invades Kuwait in July, causing the Dow to drop 18% in three months	30	1986	19.06%	
	29	1987	5.69%	
	28	1988	16.64%	
	27	1989	32%	
	26	1990	-3.42%	
	25	1991	30.95%	
	24	1992	7.60%	
	23	1993	10.17%	
	22	1994	1.19%	
	21	1995	38.02%	
70% Up 3 down years: *.com ; 9/11 and aftermath*	20	1996	23.06%	
	19	1997	33.67%	
	18	1998	28.73%	
	17	1999	21.11%	**30 Years: 11.90%**
	16	2000	-9.11%	
	15	2001	-11.98%	
	14	2002	-22.27%	
	13	2003	28.72%	
	12	2004	10.82%	
	11	2005	4.79%	**20 Years: 9.95%**
90% Up Only down 1 year: *The Great Recession*	10	2006	15.74%	
	9	2007	5.46%	
	8	2008	-37.22%	
	7	2009	27.11%	
	6	2010	14.87%	
	5	2011	2.07%	**10 Years: 9.15%**
	4	2012	15.88%	
	3	2013	32.43%	
	2	2014	13.81%	
	1	2015	1.3%	

Source: moneychimp.com | S&P 500 returns (with dividends); Compound Annual Growth Rate (Annualized Return)

Past performance is no guarantee of future performance and should not be relied upon as such; investment expenses and taxes were not considered. All guarantees are based on the financial strength and claims paying ability of the issuing insurance company.

In the last decade, only one year ended negative: 2008, the year of the Great Recession. Out of the last thirty years, only five ended negative. Look: 1986–1995 was 90% positive, 1996–2005 was 70% positive, and 2006–2015 was 90% positive. Does that surprise you?

Let's go a little further back.

How Often in the 1930s–50s Did the S&P Increase in Value?

Year	S&P Total Return (Including Dividends)	Total
1930	-24.90%	
1931	-43.34%	
1932	-8.19%	
1933	53.99%	
1934	-1.44%	
1935	47.67%	40% Up
1936	33.92%	
1937	-35.03%	
1938	31.12%	
1939	-0.41%	
1940	-9.78%	
1941	-11.59%	
1942	20.34%	
1943	25.90%	
1944	19.75%	
1945	36.44%	70% Up
1946	-8.07%	
1947	5.71%	
1948	5.50%	
1949	18.79%	
1950	31.71%	
1951	24.02%	
1952	18.37%	
1953	-0.99%	
1954	52.62%	
1955	31.56%	80% Up
1956	6.56%	
1957	-10.78%	
1958	43.36%	
1959	11.96%	

Past performance is no guarantee of future performance and should not be relied upon as such; Investment expenses and taxes were not considered.

How Often in the 1960s–90s Did the S&P Increase in Value?

Year	S&P Total Return (Including Dividends)	Total
1960	0.47%	
1961	26.89%	
1962	-8.73%	
1963	22.80%	
1964	16.48%	
1965	12.45%	70% Up
1966	-10.06%	
1967	23.98%	
1968	11.06%	
1969	-8.50%	
1970	4.01%	
1971	14.31%	
1972	18.98%	
1973	-14.66%	
1974	-26.47%	
1975	37.20%	70% Up
1976	23.84%	
1977	-7.18%	
1978	6.56%	
1979	18.44%	
1980	32.50%	
1981	-4.92%	
1982	21.55%	
1983	22.56%	
1984	6.27%	
1985	31.73%	90% Up
1986	18.67%	
1987	5.25%	
1988	16.61%	
1989	31.69%	
1990	-3.11%	
1991	30.47%	
1992	7.62%	
1993	10.08%	
1994	1.32%	
1995	37.58%	90% Up
1996	22.96%	
1997	33.36%	
1998	28.58%	
1999	21.04%	

Past performance is no guarantee of future performance and should not be relied upon as such; Investment expenses and taxes were not considered.

Look at each decade:

- 1930–1939, 40% up
- 1940–1949, 70% up
- 1950–1959, 80% up
- 1960–1969, 70% up
- 1970–1979, 70% up
- 1980–1989, 90% up
- 1990–1999, 90% up

Considering the market historically from 1930 until today, we see positive market results over 75% of the time. Only during the Great Depression era in the 1930s were there more negative years than positive years in a ten-year time frame.

Additionally, from 1930 until today only three periods of losses lasted more than two years. The large majority of the years were positive, and after any short sequence of negative years the market soon rebounded.

You might be thinking, "Wait a minute. You just said it was a challenge to predict market returns, right?" Yes, I did. And it is a challenge…over the short term. In fact, I say it's impossible. But you may see long-term trends.

Listening to the shouting on the news about recent market declines, you will find it hard to believe that the capital equity markets will consistently go up. But when you step back and look at the numbers over a multi-decade horizon, you see consistent growth with a handful of market corrections.

This consistent growth and correction reflects capitalism. It reflects ownership in companies that make profits, and you can purchase these companies' future profits. Any comparison of public equity market investments to cash or fixed income investments shows that, over time, the capital equity markets exponentially outperform the others.

The Long-Term Power of Markets

Growth of $1 — 1926 to 2015

Hypothetical value of $1 invested at the beginning of 1927 and kept invested through December 31, 2015. Assumes reinvestment of income and no transaction costs or taxes. This is for illustrative purposes only and not indicative of any investment. Total returns in U.S. dollars. Past performance is no guarantee of future results.

U.S. Large Cap Stocks represented by the SBBI U.S. Large Company Stock Index, which is an unmanaged index of stocks of large U.S. companies. The Consumer Price Indexes (CPI) program produces monthly data on changes in the prices paid by urban consumers for a representative basket of goods and services. Long-Term Government Bonds, One-Month U.S. Treasury Bills, and U.S. Consumer Price Index (inflation), source: Morningstar's 2015 Stocks, Bonds, And Inflation Yearbook (2016). Indexes are unmanaged baskets of securities than investors cannot directly invest in. Index performance does not reflect the fees or expenses associated with the management of an actual portfolio.

Risks associated with investing in stocks potentially include increased volatility (up and down movement in the value of your assets) and loss of principal. T Bills and government bonds are backed by the U.S. government and guaranteed as to the timely payment of principal and interest. T Bills and government bonds are subject to interest rate and inflation risk and their values will decline as interest rates rise.

I do believe that over the next 30 years three to five significant market corrections will occur—like those in the previous 30 years. But I also believe that new highs will follow these market corrections—as in previous periods. Historically, new highs have always occurred after downturns, in as short as five months and as long as eight years. Every major correction is always followed by a new high. If you do not believe this, you probably should not invest in the equities market at all.

The question now is not, "Should I invest?" but "Am I willing to stay invested for the long term?" Your time frame must allow you to weather the bear markets instead of selling out. You must believe in the marketplace and in capitalism. You must view your participation with a long-term horizon. You must possess the intestinal fortitude to endure market correction lows and then participate in the potential gain from market correction highs.

This may be a paradigm shift for you. We tend to be led by the constant barrage of information from the media and business reports. These all focus on the capital markets being derailed by world events: Iraq's invasion of Kuwait in 1990, Y2K in 1999, 9/11 in 2001, and widespread failure of large financial institutions in 2008. These events were major contributors to the five down years since 1986. Such events do impact the market—in the short term. The best defense against alarmist information is a long-term perspective, one that is not unnerved by real or hyped-up events.

One key strategy to help minimize your market loss in the market is to keep a long-term perspective. Ride the market long enough (probably just a few years) and you will have the potential for positive results. If you are willing to face market volatility, stay invested, and protect yourself through proper diversification, you can weather the storm and and have the potential to come out ahead in the long run. That is one key strategy to minimize your investment losses.

What if you could earn market returns without sharing in market losses? What if you could create a "floor" to your downside? You can. It is called a **capped strategy,** and it is the second strategy to minimize loss.

The capped strategy (also known as an indexed strategy) adds a "loss floor" to the bottom of your investments, though you also must accept a "growth ceiling." That is, you will never take losses from the investment, but you cannot have unlimited percentage growth in any given year. Here is an illustration to clarify the capped strategy.

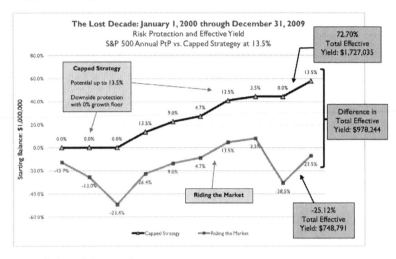

Source: Midland National Life Insurance Company

The historical performance of the S&P 500 is not intended as an indication of its future performance and is not guaranteed. This graph is only intended to demonstrate how the S&P 500, excluding dividends, would be impacted by a hypothetical growth cap of 13.5% and hypothetical growth floor of 0%, and is not a prediction of how any indexed universal life insurance product might have operated had it existed over the period depicted above. The actual historical growth cap and growth floor of an indexed universal life insurance product existing over the period depicted above may have been higher or lower than assumed, and likely would have fluctuated subject to product guarantees. This graph does not reflect the impact of life insurance policy charges.

Past performance is no guarantee of future performance and should not be relied upon as such; Investment expenses and taxes were not considered.

All guarantees are based on the financial strength and claims paying ability of the issuing insurance company.

This graph illustrates the so-called Lost Decade of 2000–2009. Suppose you had a million dollars invested with a ride-the-market strategy. Look at the bottom line on the graph: over that decade you received a negative 25.12% total effective yield. How did this occur? First, you started out badly. From 2000 until 2002 you experienced losses. In 2000 you ended up with negative 12.7%, in 2001 you suffered an agonizing 13.0% loss, and in 2002 once again you suffered with a negative 23.4% beating. Your million dollars has lost a lot of value during that first three years…looks painful.

Then the market began recovering like it always does. From 2003 through 2007 the market had positive results. After the low, you gained anywhere from 3.5% to 26.4% by riding the market through the volatility. In 2007, you finally ended up with almost as much as you started the decade with. Nice!

But then the big, bad year of 2008 hit you with a 38.5% loss. Next, 2009 rebounded with a positive 23.5%. Even though 23.5% sounds good, it was not enough to make up for the 38.5% hit. That's because it would take a 64.9% return to get you back to your high water mark.

Think about it this way. If you had a million dollars and lost 50%, how much would you have left? Easy: $500,000. How much more money until you regain the million? Another $500,000. The rate of return required on your half a million dollars to regain the other half a million is 100%. (Fun with numbers!) The point is that losses, and making up for losses, can be very costly to your wealth.

During the Lost Decade, your million dollars eroded to $748,791. That is a negative 25.12% total effective yield. You stayed in through the Lost Decade, and in the end, you lost. In fact you lost $251,209. The good news is that like all crashes, the market recovered to a new high. Between the years of 2012 and 2013 you recovered your million dollars and from there went on to reach new highs and created significant gains (That is if you stayed in the market, didn't panic, and sell your positions). That is riding the market.

Contrast those results with the results of a capped strategy. In this strategy, your account is credited based on an index. The rate of return ranges, with a cap on the upside (ceiling) and a cap on the downside (floor).

So now you invest the same million dollars in the year 2000, but this time you use a capped strategy. During 2000 and 2002 your million dollars does not grow, because the market experienced losses. However, your account responds to the negative market simply by giving you zero crediting—you suffer no loss. You still have a million dollars! Then in 2003–2007, the market gained and you gained along with it. But your growth was capped, for sake of example at 13.5%. This means that the market may have performed better than 13.5% during any of those years, but your maximum allowable growth is 13.5%. Not quite as nice, but remember—you are not susceptible to losses.

Because you risk nothing, you lose nothing in 2008 when the market drops 38.5%. Your capped strategy turns a 38.5% loss into a comparative gain—everyone else is now at the bottom of a hole, but you're still up on top.

In 2009 the market rebounds 23.5%; however, since your cap is set at 13.5% you only realize a 13.5% gain. That's not much fun. But remember: You get 13.5% **of your original million dollars!** Not 13.5% of the substantially reduced amount others had remaining after the 2008 crash.

Over the Lost Decade, your million dollars invested with a capped strategy grew to $1,727,035. That is a 72.7% total effective yield—fantastic. In one of the worst investment decades in recent history, you realized a 72.7% gain with the indexing strategy.

If you look back at the comparative illustration, you will see that the capped strategy emerged from the Lost Decade with $978,244 more than the ride-the-market strategy. This illustrates the power of **minimizing loss.**

Substantially reducing your risk of loss includes two main steps:

1. Own a diversified market portfolio, invested for the long term.

2. Invest your low to moderate-risk funds using a capped strategy.

The combination of these two strategies leaves you with a good amount of upside potential while protecting you against excessive loss. The market portfolio can realize incredible gains, but is susceptible to market volatility. The capped strategy is steady, and while it does not gain as quickly, it will prevent downside losses in your portfolio. Combining these two principles can create somewhat predictable wealth.

How do you get these capped returns? One approach is through the crediting mechanism of the permanent life insurance contracts discussed earlier. Indexed Universal Life insurance contracts grant this unique opportunity. The crediting strategy empowers doctors to maximize their investment returns, minimize their downside risk, and obtain the tax benefits of insurance.

Let's look at one more example, using the horrible decade of the Great Depression.

Year	S&P Total Return including dividends	Ride The Market	The Market w/ a floor: and a ceiling of:	0.00% / 13.5%	Year
		$ 1,000,000	$ 1,000,000		
1930	-24.90%	751,000	1,000,000	0.00%	1930
1931	-43.34%	425,517	1,000,000	0.00%	1931
1932	-8.19%	390,667	1,000,000	0.00%	1932
1933	53.99%	601,588	1,135,000	13.50%	1933
1934	-1.44%	592,925	1,135,000	0.00%	1934
1935	47.67%	875,572	1,288,225	13.50%	1935
1936	33.92%	1,172,566	1,462,135	13.50%	1936
1937	-35.03%	761,816	1,462,135	0.00%	1937
1938	31.12%	998,894	1,659,524	13.50%	1938
1939	-0.41%	994,798	1,659,524	0.00%	1939
Change in Value:		-0.52%	65.95%		

Difference in Value
$664,726

Source: moneychimp.com | S&P 500 returns (with dividends); Compound Annual Growth Rate (Annualized Return)

The investor who invested a million dollars in the market from 1930 until 1939 had a negative 0.52% change in value. The million dollars shrunk to $994,798. Not great, but not horrible. This decade was a wild ride, staying in the market rewarded the investor with only a minimal loss.

The second investor used the capped strategy. He grew his million dollars to $1,659,524 for a 65.95% return! This was during the **worst ten years of investing** in the modern history of the market.

Hopefully you can see how strategic investment planning can impact your future. I make no claims to clairvoyance about the stock market; my advice is intended to grow your wealth irrespective of it. Whether a bull market or a bear market, your money should grow and not shrink.

As an investor, consider employing both strategies above to minimize your losses. Invest in the market broadly with a diversified portfolio, and consider using a capped strategy to further minimize loss in your portfolio for down markets. This approach will let you in on the significant long-term market upside, while protecting your financial future from the downside.

Investment principle #2 – Invest passively

Few people understand how active and passive investing differ. But if you lack comprehension here, you may shoot yourself in the foot.

In an **active investing** style you pick individual stocks and try to time the market. You search out internal analytics, unique insights, and market inefficiencies. You believe your research can put you ahead of the average investor. The goal? Beat the market by attaining as high a rate of return as possible.

Almost the entire financial services industry revolves around active investing. Media reports and financial gurus condition us to believe that advisors and investment managers have special knowledge. Supposedly, they have the unique insight and enhanced skillset needed to seize better returns. We assume they understand market timing and market movements—at least, understand them better than the average individual investor. The financial media wants us to believe that active portfolio management will improve our gains. That is the premise of trying to beat the market.

The second style is **passive investing.** This is also called "owning the market," which means your portfolio consists of widely diversified securities representing the entire market. Instead of placing your entire investment nest egg into only a few companies, you spread it out over thousands of companies. This diversified portfolio should mimic the general returns of the entire market.

When you initially establish your portfolio, you need to determine your asset allocation—that is, how much of your investment you put in equities (stocks) and how much you put in fixed income (bonds). Your allocation should be based on your risk tolerance and unique situation.

Then you are done. That's it. No more checking stock reports daily, no more frantic buying and selling. Just stop.

You leave your portfolio alone, only changing the allocation when your life situation changes. Of course, as markets change your portfolio may need rebalancing to stay consistent with your asset allocation model.

With passive investing, you forget about timing the market. You ignore shifting in and out of asset classes. You reject chasing that hot stock your colleague has been promoting. Aside from the benefit of lower costs due to lower portfolio turnover, you position yourself to benefit from long-term market returns. You stick to the belief that over time, future returns will be positive. Remember the results from 1930 until today? The market produced positive returns over 75% of the time. Capture these returns for your wealth accumulation.

What does history tell us about active versus passive investing? Moving beyond vague feelings and hearsay, what say the facts?

Percentage of Active Funds that Outperformed their Index 2009 – 2013

Percentage of Active Funds that Outperformed their Index 2009–2013

Source: Standard & Poor's Indices Versus Active Funds Scorecard (SPIVA), 2013. Index used for comparison: US Equities —S&P 1500 Index; International —S&P 700 Index; Emerging Markets —S&P/IFCI Composite; US Fixed —GovLong, Global Fixed —Global Income Funds. Outperformance is based upon equal weight fund counts. For illustrative purposes only. Index returns do not include payment of any sales charges or fees an investor would pay to purchase the securities they represent. Such costs would lower performance. Past performance is not an indication of future results. More recent performance may alter these assessments or outcomes.

Source: http://fpanebraska.com/downloads/fpa_of_nebraska_september_2014_meeting_loring_ward_presentation.pdf

This chart records the percentage of actively managed funds that *outperformed* their index over a five-year period. If you invest in an actively managed fund, and it outperforms the index, congratulations. You have earned more money than you would have by merely investing in the index and waiting five years.

What percentage of actively managed funds do outperform the index? Look at the leftmost bar on the chart above: U.S. Equities. The chart indicates that from 2009–2013, actively managed U.S. equities beat their indexes 39% of the time. On the flip side, it indicates that active managers failed to beat the market 61% of the time. That is, they either performed identically or fared worse! Three out of five times, you would be better off investing passively in the market index.

This holds true for international markets, emerging markets, and fixed income markets. Examine the rest of the chart. The premise that active management can consistently beat the market does not at all hold true.

You might have a clever idea at this point: "I will find an active manager who is part of the 39%. I will locate outperforming funds, invest my money with them, and come out ahead." Good thought, but the execution may not turn out so well. Check out this next illustration:

Can Past Performance Predict Future Results?

10-Year Annualized Performance of 934
U.S. Equity Funds vs. S&P 500 1999–2008

529 Funds Outperform S&P 500

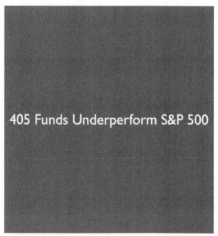

405 Funds Underperform S&P 500

Data source: Center for Research in Security Prices (CRSP), For illustrative purposes only. Mutual funds were placed in descending order of 10-year annualized performance, and subsequent 5-year performance assumes the same ordering as the 10- year period. The number of funds for the subsequent 5-year period represent existing funds from the 10- year period. Eligible universe is share classes of US Equity Open End mutual funds domiciled in the US with prospectus benchmark of the S&P 500, classified into the US Stock mutual fund asset class by Morningstar Direct with a ten-year annualized return as of Dec. 31, 2008 in Morningstar Direct.

This illustration measures the 10-year performance of 934 U.S. equity funds in comparison to the performance of the S&P 500. Out of 934 funds, 529 outperformed the S&P and 405 underperformed.

You look at these results and decide to put your money into some of the top-performing equity funds. Fast forward five years—look at this next illustration.

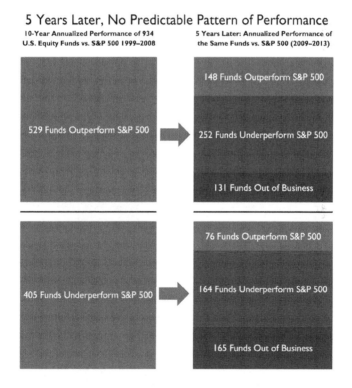

5 Years Later, No Predictable Pattern of Performance

10-Year Annualized Performance of 934 U.S. Equity Funds vs. S&P 500 1999–2008

5 Years Later: Annualized Performance of the Same Funds vs. S&P 500 (2009–2013)

529 Funds Outperform S&P 500

148 Funds Outperform S&P 500

252 Funds Underperform S&P 500

131 Funds Out of Business

405 Funds Underperform S&P 500

76 Funds Outperform S&P 500

164 Funds Underperform S&P 500

165 Funds Out of Business

Data source: Center for Research in Security Prices (CRSP), For illustrative purposes only. Mutual funds were placed in descending order of 10-year annualized performance, and subsequent 5-year performance assumes the same ordering as the 10- year period. The number of funds for the subsequent 5-year period represent existing funds from the 10- year period. Eligible universe is share classes of US Equity Open End mutual funds domiciled in the US with prospectus benchmark of the S&P 500, classified into the US Stock mutual fund asset class by Morningstar Direct with a ten-year annualized return as of Dec. 31, 2008 in Morningstar Direct. Mutual fund universe statistical data provided by Morningstar, Inc.; Indices are not available for direct investment; therefore, their performance does not reflect the expenses associated with the management of an actual portfolio. Past performance is no guarantee of future results, and there is always the risk that an investor may lose money. S&P 500® is a registered trademark of Standard & Poor's Financial Services LLC 2013. All investments involve risk, including loss of principal.

http://fpanebraska.com/downloads/fpa_of_nebraska _september_2014_meeting_loring_ward_ presentati on.pdf

How did your outperforming funds rank against the S&P 500? Only 146 of the 529 outperforming funds repeated their success. Another 252 funds underperformed, and 131 funds went out of business.

Past performance does not guarantee future results. That saying is a financial cliché, yet very true. Previous success is no predictor of future success. Attempting to actively invest and pick a winning stock based on history is a recipe for failure. Even if you believe in active management, how could you hope to select the active managers who will consistently outperform? The odds are against you.

This is the challenge of individual investors. In this light, investing passively begins to make more sense. Compare the lackluster results of active investing to the earlier discussion on the S&P 500 performance over the last 40 years. Why risk missing out on the growth of the market? Why play the active game?

Here are some more hard numbers. How are average individual investors really doing?

Average Investor vs. Major Indices 1994 - 2013

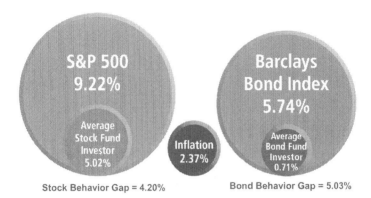

S&P 500
9.22%

Average Stock Fund Investor 5.02%

Inflation 2.37%

Barclays Bond Index 5.74%

Average Bond Fund Investor 0.71%

Stock Behavior Gap = 4.20%   Bond Behavior Gap = 5.03%

Average stock investor and average bond investor performances were used from a DALBAR study, Quantitative Analysis of Investor Behavior (QAIB), 03/2014. QAIB calculates investor returns as the change in assets after excluding sales, redemptions, and exchanges. This method of calculation captures realized and unrealized capital gains, dividends, interest, trading costs, sales charges, fees, expenses, and any other costs. After calculating investor returns in dollar terms (above), two percentages are calculated: Total investor return rate for the period and annualized investor return rate. Total return rate is determined by calculating the investor return dollars as a percentage of the net of the sales, redemptions, and exchanges for the period. The fact that buy-and-hold has been a successful strategy in the past does not guarantee that it will continue to be successful in the future. S&P 500 returns do not take into consideration any fees.

http://fpanebraska.com/downloads/fpa_of_nebraska_september_2014_meeting_loring_ward_presentation.pdf

From 1994 to 2013, the S&P 500 was up 9.22%. The average individual stock investor was up only 5%. In other words, average investors did not perform as well as the general market. The same holds true in the bond market: the overall index was up 5.74%, while the average bond investor was up only 0.71%.

These numbers show that individual investors underperform the general market just like active managers. You can invest yourself and underperform, or you can pick an active manager and still underperform.

With these odds in mind, review the equities market's positive returns in 25 out of the last 30 years. The market is up over 75% of the time. Buying into a representation of the entire market and winning over time makes sense. Plus, this frees you from spending exorbitant amounts of time and energy buying and selling individual stocks to time the market.

What happens if you try to time the market? Consider the daily returns of the Dow Jones Industrial Average (DJIA) from 1991 to 2015. A $1,000 investment over that period would grow to $12,016 (assuming dividend reinvestment). But if you were out of the market on the 10 best days, your $1,000 investment would grow to just $6,141. This illustrates the value of staying in the markets for the long run, rather than jumping in and out.

You win as long as you have time to be invested in the market long-term. In contrast, if you have a short time frame and thus cannot withstand market fluctuations and volatility, you probably should not invest in the equities market. You should pick a safe investment. Either way, the active game—trying to pick individual stocks and beat the market—is not a winning game.

A little investing psychology

Take a few minutes with this illustration. Here's how people will get themselves into trouble playing the market.

The thick line on the graph represents the market. It goes up; it goes down; it goes up again. Along the bottom you see emotions associated with the various peaks and valleys of riding the market. These emotions arise from the human brain's wiring to desire gain and avoid loss.

As the market goes up, the associated emotions are optimism, excitement, and elation. These emotions stimulate you to buy. You think, "The market performance is great. I want to participate in this. I'm going to miss the boat if I do not get on board. I need to invest!"

The truth is rather different. As the market rises toward a new high, it approaches the point of greatest potential risk. Statistical-

Investment Principle #2
Emotion often leads to trying to time markets

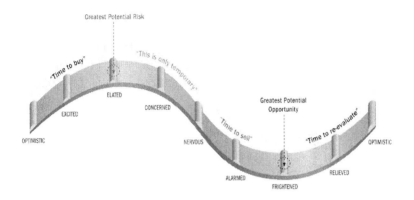

ly, you understand that the market cannot rise forever. The higher it goes, the greater the likelihood of correction and decline. This is the wrong time to invest, because downturn is imminent. But you listened to your excited emotions and invested.

Now the market starts going down. Your emotions change: you are concerned, nervous, alarmed, and frightened. Emotional drops follow market drops. Your feelings begin telling you to get out and avoid further loss. Initially, you think the correction might be only temporary—so you ride it out. Later you become alarmed and frightened. You decide, "I can't take this. I'm going to lose everything." You sell out.

But this is the worst time to sell! The bottom of the trough is the point of greatest potential for the market to recover. As you intellectually know the market cannot rise forever, you know it cannot drop forever. Sooner or later the indices will rise, and you obviously want to be on board when that happens. However, since you sold out, you are going to miss out on all the growth.

We see these trends repeat in historical data. Unfortunately, the human brain's wiring pushes us to act in these ways. We instinctively protect ourselves from perceived loss. Emotions obscure and override the facts every time, if allowed to. Largely because of this, individual investors underperform the market. They buy at the wrong time and they sell at the wrong time. They focus on the real-time gain or loss, not the 30-year horizon. Objectivity is nearly impossible.

Excellent returns come not by timing the market and picking stocks for the short term. Rather, they come by diligently practicing two significant yet counterintuitive investment principles:

○ Minimize loss. You can accomplish this riding the market and staying invested for the long term. Additionally, you can minimize loss by employing a capped strategy that sets a floor and ceiling to your returns. Focus on market returns and limiting downside.

○ Invest passively. In place of active investing, practice passive investing by owning the whole market and committing to the long view. Stay objective and stick to the facts. Do not let your emotions override your brain.

If you employ these strategies, you will not underperform the market. Who knows—you may even beat it!

Concept #3.

Leaving Assets Unprotected

Doctors have lots of assets. You probably have lots of assets. But too often, doctors fail to recognize all the assets they possess. And even if they do recognize them, they unwittingly leave them unprotected.

A few definitions

What are assets? As a practitioner, you have two groups of assets: practice and personal.

Your practice assets include your medical or dental office, the equipment, and the real estate. Basically, these are any things associated with your business.

Your personal assets include your home, your car, your bank accounts, your investment accounts, and other personal possessions.

What is asset protection? The simple definition of asset protection is "the creation of ownership strategies permissible by law to secure your assets from creditor attachment." Each state has laws in place that you can use to shield your assets from creditors. This is simply using the law to its fullest extent for your greatest benefit.

You need to proactively protect your assets. Consider the analogy of homestead exemptions for property taxes on your home: tax breaks are available, but only if you file for them. The same is true for using legal asset protection. You only get it if you set it up.

To fully protect your assets, you need to be knowledgeable about what your state laws permit and forbid. Then you can set up legal structures to stand between you and potential creditors. Placing your assets under the right structures will erect a barrier, limiting or removing creditors' economic incentive to go after your assets. This may also increase your ability to force a favorable settlement if you are sued.

When you begin establishing an asset protection plan, you need to look at your entire financial situation. You should consider all your personal and business assets (and liabilities). The goal is to integrate your current tax situation, your estate planning, and your asset protection planning into a single comprehensive plan. Erecting asset protection barriers in isolation from your other financial holdings is useless; any change to the structure of your business or personal assets impacts your overall plan.

Proper asset protection is proactive, not reactive. Many doctors recognize they need asset protection. They know they need to separate personal from professional assets. However, they think they can delay until trouble arises. With no risk in sight and no creditors on the horizon, they put asset protection off. They plan to start protecting their assets in the moment of crisis.

Unfortunately, asset protection does not work that way. The law states that if you have a known creditor, and you restructure your affairs to disallow that creditor access to your assets, it does not count. This is known as an act of *fraudulent conveyance*. The courts can negate your new structure, just as though you had never made the changes.

You need to have your legal arrangements in place for a certain amount of time before a liability issue arises. Transferring your assets after you've been named in a suit or identified by a creditor is considered fraudulent.

What are the practice risks?

Risks associated with a dental or medical practice include both well-known and less familiar threats. Malpractice lawsuits are an obvious risk to physicians. If a patient has a bad outcome—whether your fault or not—that patient could potentially sue both you personally and your practice. Most medical practitioners have malpractice insurance coverage to protect against this.

Another practice risk is audit risk. Most healthcare practices are not paid directly by the patient. Rather, they are paid by a third party—usually an insurance company or the government. If any questions arise regarding your billing practices, the third party payer can come in and audit your books. This payer may be the federal government, the state government, or an insurance company. If your billing practices were in error, your practice is at risk. Typically, you cannot purchase insurance against this risk. You are forced to divert resources and time to cooperate with the audit, which can rack up quite a cost.

You also have the risk of someone questioning your license. Healthcare professionals are licensed state by state; if someone files a complaint against you with a state agency, your license could be suspended. You are then subject to proceedings and hearings regarding your competency to practice. And if you are rendered unable to practice due to a suspended or revoked license, you become unable to generate revenue.

Do not deceive yourself by thinking you can avoid this risk through upright conduct. No factual basis is necessary for these accusations—I have witnessed physicians and dentists being dragged through the mud on spurious, ridiculous, incredulous charges. However, the process to clear your good name is so long and bureaucratic that you can lose months (if not years) of revenue. The system is skewed against practitioners; doctors are often considered guilty until proven innocent. The potential financial drain is real. The reputational risk is real. Recovering from both may take years, as you must reestablish your entire patient base.

The newest risk rearing its ugly head comes with the advent of electronic medical records. Requirements to ensure patient confidentiality are placed upon providers. Even small potential breaches of privacy can impact your business. Doctors and their staff must follow prescribed protocols regarding how patient information is handled. Cyber security is a huge risk.

Incidents in all these risk areas are increasing, in my experience. And these are only the top anticipated risks to your practice. Many additional risks exist which we cannot even fathom. Your potential risk is limited only by the creativity of starving plaintiff attorneys.

What are the personal risks?

Many doctors who clearly understand their practice risks ignore their personal risks. Personal risks include tort claims such as falls and traffic accidents. For instance: If someone walks onto your real estate property, trips over a one-inch sidewalk crack, and injures himself, he could sue you. Or maybe you have kids just starting to drive. I do. It terrifies me! They are very responsible drivers, but they do not yet have the experience to understand how dangerous it is out there behind the wheel.

A few years ago, my son was involved in a minor fender bender. His car was not even damaged and the police report was uneventful. Nonetheless, two years after the mishap my family was served legal documents claiming $1 million for pain and suffering. Most accidents occur for drivers between ages 16 and 25, according to insurance companies. If your minor child drives a car titled in your name, you are at risk and your assets are at risk. How any piece of personal property is titled substantially affects the reach of lawsuits.

Doctors are frequently pursued to invest in the next great real estate deal, development deal, or business startup. Enterprising individuals secure loans or capital to start their venture, then find a physician to sign a personal guarantee—because a doctor's finances and income streams are secure. But signing a personal guarantee, even alongside other investors, could prove a devastating risk to your livelihood. If the project goes belly up, the bank looks to the most financially stable guarantor to make them whole. You could be on the hook for the whole liability. Doctors should never sign personal guarantees if they can at all help it. If forced to sign a guarantee, make sure that you understand your potential exposure and take steps to minimize the risk.

A third personal risk is the claims of your children's or parents' creditors. Suppose you co-sign on your kid's credit card, car, or school loan. Suppose you are caring for your parents and have assumed some financial responsibility. Should your child or parent not pay, you could find yourself on the hook for their expenses.

Finally, the dreaded IRS could decide to audit you. Or some other governmental agency could decide to investigate your personal affairs. In all these ways and more, your personal assets are at risk.

Achieving asset protection

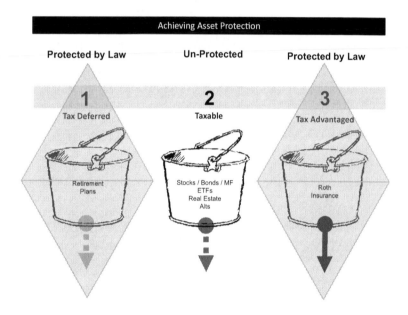

Remember this graph? Earlier we talked at length about the tax benefits of bucket #1, the Tax Deferred bucket. There are also additional benefits of using this bucket. One is that qualified retirement plans are protected assets, and therefore not exposed to creditors. A good asset protection plan typically includes maximal participation in a retirement plan suiting your goals and needs.

Above, we briefly discussed comprehensive planning. The idea is that you need to look at your retirement and investment planning holistically, not with each aspect in isolation. This illustrates why. Connecting your retirement investment vehicle to your asset protection needs results in a double benefit. The bucket of tax-deferred options offers tax benefits, and also erects a barrier around your personal assets against risk and creditors.

Look now at bucket #3, the Tax Advantaged bucket. Remember the incredible tax benefits in this bucket? It provides great asset protection as well. Indexed universal life insurance policies and annuities are protected assets in twenty-seven states. You can have tax-deferred growth and tax-free access, protected from potential creditors. What a deal!

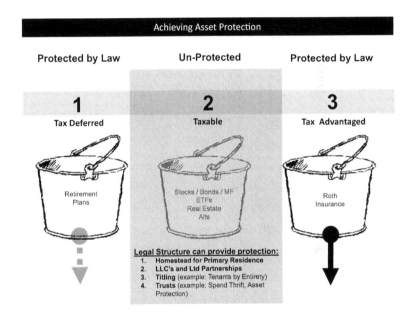

In certain states, your primary residence is protected from creditors under the homestead laws. This is a powerful asset protector if you are lucky enough to live in one of these states.

Please note that laws regarding asset-protection options and structures vary by state. Most must be set up by lawyers. Include a qualified asset protection and estate planning attorney in the development of your plan.

The illustration above includes several other legal structures to provide you some level of creditor protection. These structures can be broken down into business entities (like LLCs or Limited Partnerships), titling issues (like tenants by the entirety), or trusts (like spendthrift or asset protection trusts).

As previously mentioned, you need to consider all the options in concert with your investment, tax, and estate planning strategy. The specifics of your practice, your family, your goals, and your location influence which options are best for you.

Some solutions are obvious. Some will require you to make an educated decision, based on your strategic objectives. Each has advantages and disadvantages—for instance, cost and complexity of setting up a structure, limited access to a fund, or less control. But the advantages of tax minimization and risk mitigation are often worth it. The calculation is a balancing act between risks and rewards.

Asset protection is not as simple as saying "You should participate in a trust" or "You should put your money in retirement plans." A decision has numerous nuances and implications, each of which affects the next decision. You must seek to understand the wider impacts. Find an advisor who will approach your planning with both a macro and micro focus. This requires a comprehensive team approach, which we will explore further in the next concept.

Concept #4.

Missing the Big Picture

Lots of doctors miss the big picture. As explained in the last chapter, financial planning that will truly secure your assets and ensure your future must address every aspect of your finances, both personal and professional. This includes your income and retirement plan, your tax strategies, your investment strategies, your asset protection, and more. Each potential move should be evaluated in terms of its implications for your goals.

Every decision that you make impacts other aspects of your planning. You must grasp the overall plan and refuse to make decisions in isolation. A piecemeal approach may work when ordering an à la carte dinner, but is doomed to fail when developing a comprehensive financial life plan.

Much financial planning is simply uncoordinated. But in addition, another part of the big picture is rarely recognized by the financial services marketplace—even by those who offer "comprehensive" financial planning. This is the concept of **different stages of life** planning. Financial planning is not just about managing investments, not just about insurance, not just about saving money. Comprehensive planning encompasses all decisions about money: It includes *spending* as well as saving.

Offering "comprehensive financial planning" is nice, but not very many planners differentiate between the **accumulation phase** and the **distribution phase** of your financial life. These two phases of your financial life are illustrated in the graph below showing a doctors' economic life cycle.

Doctors' economic life cycle

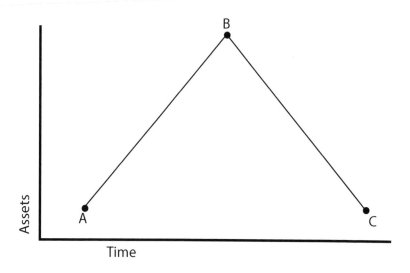

During a doctor's career, financial earnings follow the pattern on this graph. The first point on the graph is Point A, a significant milestone in your career. This is when you are earning more money than you are spending to live. You have paid your bills and still have something left over. At this stage, you have surplus earnings or discretionary income. You can spend this income to improve your lifestyle, pay down debt, or invest. Now you need to start thinking about financial planning.

Point A can occur at any age for a doctor. Typically, you can start saving significant amounts somewhere in your 30s. Doctors tend to reach Point A later than those in most other professions. Reasons for this include the length of training, which is anywhere from 4 to 12 years after college. Additionally, this training normally requires extensive funding through loans. Many doctors have six figures of debt before they enter the work force and begin earning a salary. Due to this delayed start, doctors have a compressed earnings cycle time frame. For this reason, making the right choices early on can have an enormous impact on a doctor's success. That is worth repeating: Making the right choices about money early on can have an enormous impact on a doctor's success.

Early mistakes may never be fully recovered from. You simply do not have time to make up for poor decisions. The time value of money and compounding interest depend on time to overcome bad choices.

If you have not yet reached Point A (making more than you spend), then you do not need comprehensive financial planning. You need to do two things.

First, you probably need to increase your income by examining how you run your business and tightening up the ship with efficient practice management strategies. This is not personal financial planning but practice management. You need to figure out how to increase your top line revenue.

The second thing you can do is on the other side of the profit equation: You probably need to decrease your expenses. While you are studying efficient practice management and increasing revenue, you need to evaluate your spending. As a financial adage says, "It is not what you earn but what you keep that matters." Controlling your spending and living within your means is probably the most important contributor to financial success. Stop up the leaking gaps of expenses. You need to reach Point A and have more money coming in than going out. To attain Point A—which is where all good financial planning begins—your personal revenue must exceed personal expenditures.

Note that these two efforts of increasing income and decreasing expenses apply to both your professional and personal life. It is very possible to run a tight ship with your business, but be floundering at home. Or vice versa.

Eventually, with some effort you will reach Point A. Now you have the wonderful choice of how to spend your surplus dollars. There are three options: You can spend more, you can pay down debt, or you can invest. This decision is what financial planning is all about. Most doctors elect for a combination of all three. As you take your surplus and allocate some of it to investing, you begin to save money over time, year in and year out. This money compounds. After a number of years, your assets accumulate to reach the second point on the graph, Point B.

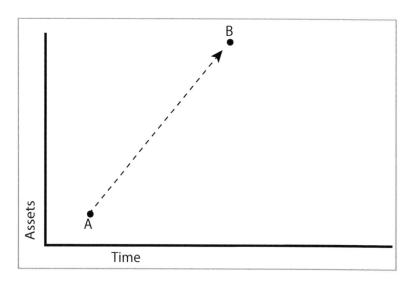

Point B is the point at which your accumulated assets are sufficient to fund your lifestyle throughout your remaining life expectancy. In other words, you have enough money to quit working. You do not have to quit working if you do not want to, but you can. Income for your daily expenses is now generated from your savings and from asset liquidation. Point B for many is called *retirement*. It's financial freedom. No longer do you work for income; income is generated from your accumulated assets.

The line from Point A to Point B is the **accumulation phase.** Accumulation planning focuses on how to maximize the growth of your surplus. Ideally, each year you will invest your discretionary income into assets you have purchased in previous years.

During this period, you consider how your money is invested, whether you are getting a favorable rate of return, and how to protect one of your most important assets: yourself. More specifically, your ability to continue to work and earn an income. Protection from premature death or disability is essential. Mitigate your risks with insurance and asset protection strategies. All these issues belong integrally to accumulation planning. The return on your assets will grow over time, ultimately building up to Point B.

There is a final point on this graph of the doctor's economic life cycle. It is Point C: end of life. From Point B to Point C, you distribute your principal, savings, and earnings to fund your lifestyle. This is the **distribution phase.**

During the distribution phase, your preoccupations differ widely from all that consumed you in the accumulation phase. Now you want to protect yourself against long-term care and healthcare expenses. You want to secure your assets. You want to diminish your investment risk level to protect your market gains. You want to ensure your income will permit you to continue your desired lifestyle throughout your remaining years. Perhaps you desire to give some of your assets to your family, or to organizations that support your cherished values. Additionally, you need to establish structures to ensure your legacy wishes are carried out. If you do not complete the legal footwork for your legacy wishes via estate planning, your assets are at risk.

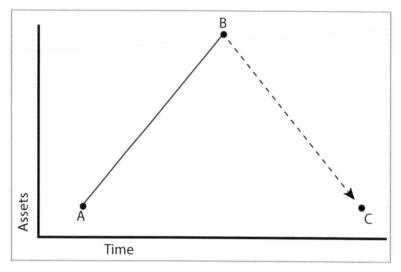

From Point B to C the line is trending downward. This represents a decrease in your net worth. You will liquidate your assets during the distribution phase, either by spending them or giving them away. Absent these actions your assets will be taken away.

Taxation is one way your assets are taken away. If you don't plan correctly during distribution, your estate can erode due to taxation. One goal of a comprehensive financial plan is to ensure that the wealth you worked for your whole life ends up being used to leave a legacy. I do not have many doctors that desire to endow the government.

As you can see, distribution planning is very different from accumulation planning. Comprehensive financial planning begins with the accumulation phase. It aims to bring you to Point B, the point of financial independence. Once you hit Point B, your financial decisions will primarily focus on establishing your life legacy. These two phases are each unique. They require different perspectives and utilize different planning tools.

Financial planners strive to get clients to Point B—preferably before Point C arrives! Would you like to spend many years of your life in the distribution phase? Though reaching Point B is crucial, the time spent between Points B and C is often one of the most rewarding periods in a person's life. Here you dream and live big. You define what your life means and what it will mean to future generations. You engage in a life well lived—a life that will be remembered. The joy of participating in both economic life cycle phases brings meaning to my clients, and to me as a financial life planner.

The doctors' economic life cycle serves as the framework for comprehensive financial planning. Are you in the accumulation phase or the distribution phase? Do you know what your priorities should be for each phase? Do you understand which priorities trump others? Where would you start? Maybe you do not know. That is where a comprehensive financial planner comes in.

Multitudinous industry providers use the term "comprehensive planning" or "holistic planning." What does this mean? It changes depending on whom you ask. Banks, insurance companies, brokers, and other investment managers all use this phrase loosely. How do you discern if they are an expert or merely a smooth talker? How do you avoid becoming a victim of financial marketers? How do you not miss the big picture?

The C.U.R.E.

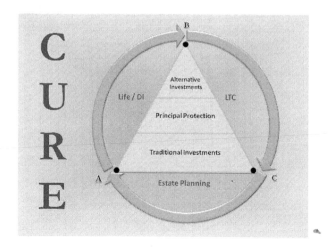

After practicing medicine for a decade myself, I developed a comprehensive planning process for doctors. It deals with the essential four areas that are the primary components of a comprehensive plan. I call it the C.U.R.E. process. Each letter represents one of the four cornerstones of planning, which address the needs you have in all phases of your economic life cycle—both accumulation and distribution. These four areas address all of a doctor's financial planning needs. Following it, you can rest assured your plan is complete.

The C.U.R.E. process is not the only one available, but is unique in that it is designed for you, a doctor. I use it for my own family's planning.

One of my primary goals in the creation of this process has been paving the way for doctors to regain peace of mind and focus. You could consult multiple advisors, lawyers, accountants, insurance agents, and brokers—each of whom would advise you from within the silo of their expertise. However, those narrow areas of expertise rarely overlap with each other in beneficial ways unless someone deliberately intervenes. We might call that "someone" a trusted advocate.

I believe that working with a single trusted advocate, who understands your overall goals, is the key to managing your financial planning. Instead of spending your time managing a cadre of advisors, wouldn't you prefer working with one professional who coordinates all the pieces? Wouldn't you like to free up your time for professional activities and personal recreation? Wouldn't this restore your focus and peace of mind, so that you can pour yourself into your family and your patients and your personal priorities?

The C.U.R.E. comprises issues particular to your profession that another financial planner's approach might miss. I have used and tweaked this process for 25 years, and find that it resonates with healthcare professionals.

The C.U.R.E represents the four components of planning:

- C. Comprehensive (structure)
- U. Unexpected risk (insurance)
- R. Ratio or recipe (investments)
- E. Estate (estate and asset protection)

Let's take a closer look at the C.U.R.E. components now.

C. Comprehensive (structure)

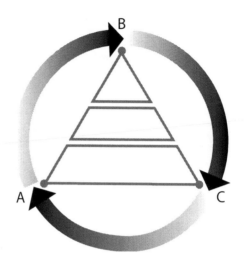

The C stands for **Comprehensive**, or Complete, as in "the complete picture." Predominately, these issues relate to how your personal and business assets are structured. The C.U.R.E. process begins with my team and I working to understand the big picture:

○ What are your assets?

○ How are they titled?

○ What are your practice assets and your personal assets?

○ Do you have any investment accounts or retirement plans?

○ What is the status of your home?

○ What buckets are your investments in, and what are the tax implications?

○ What are your liabilities?

○ What is the structure of your practice?

○ What financial life goals do you want to fund?

○ What unique needs and wants do you have? Maybe you need to provide lifetime care for a special needs child. Or perhaps you dream about starting a free healthcare clinic in Sub-Saharan Africa after you retire in the States.

Each physician and dentist I work with sketches out an individual picture. Every set of assets and liabilities is different. Every long-term dream and retirement goal is special. Thus, it is critical to work with an advisor who values taking time to understand you and to help you articulate your aims.

Have you ever worked on a jigsaw puzzle? If so, you know putting 1,000 pieces together is quite challenging. Here is a question: What is the most important piece of that puzzle? The sides? The corner?

The most important piece of the puzzle is the box cover. Only that picture of the completed puzzle tells you what you are creating. As the puzzle box picture helps you assemble the puzzle, so the big picture helps you organize your financial life. In isolation, puzzle pieces are worthless. They do not make sense. But when you see a single piece in relation to the complete picture, you know exactly how it fits. Individual financial products are ineffective unless you can see the financial life picture you are trying to create. That is the essence of the first cornerstone of planning, the C.

U. Unexpected risks (insurance)

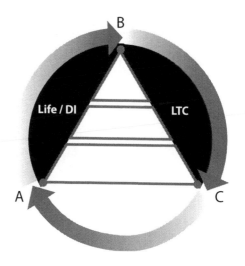

The second component of a sound comprehensive plan is risk mitigation. This is our next cornerstone, represented by the U in C.U.R.E.

The U stands for **unexpected risks.** These are risks you can prepare for with insurance vehicles:

- O life
- O health
- O disability
- O business overhead
- O property and casualty
- O liability
- O long-term care

Obtaining appropriate insurance to protect yourself against unexpected events is essential. From Point A to Point B in your economic life cycle—the accumulation phase—you need to protect your most important asset: your ability to earn an income. Early in your career, your ability to earn is a more important asset than your house, investment accounts, or 401K. Your education and training has made a professional with an earning capacity of millions of dollars. Protecting this potential is a must.

Protecting against premature death or disability with life and disability insurance is also a top priority. You need to guarantee that if something compromised your ability to earn, your family would be provided for.

During your accumulation phase, you also want adequate coverage against risks to your practice. These include business overhead, malpractice, and property and casualty, with umbrella insurance for other assets you may have.

Between Points B and C lies the distribution phase of your life cycle. When you are retired and possibly no longer earning an income, you should consider long-term care insurance. You have accumulated all the assets you will ever need. Financial freedom is yours. Now protect those assets.

As a health care professional, you have personally experienced the possibilities. Permanent disability, Alzheimer's disease, strokes, and similar conditions require expensive assistance. Financial freedom means your assets cover *normal* daily activities during your life expectancy. However: If you, your spouse, or another dependent has an *abnormal* and unexpected medical issue, the cost of such an event could erode your estate and put your retirement plans at risk. Distribution planning must include a conversation about long-term care insurance. Funding for this possibility is a must, whether through an insurance policy or self-insurance.

I get it—this is a lot of insurance. Many doctors become a little uncomfortable or defensive when this topic comes up. However, it is critical to realize how one unexpected risk occurrence can completely decimate every asset in your financial stable. Risk mitigation is one of the essential cornerstones of a well-thought-out financial plan.

Also, do not forget the benefits available in certain life insurance policies. Besides the death benefit, living benefits can be generated. Some life insurance policies can act as a tax- free, asset-protected income source with market-like returns, no downside loss, tax-deferred growth, and access at any point. Remember the discussion of the tax benefits in concept 1, the investment benefits in concept 2, and the asset protection benefits in concept 3. You can see how truly integrated all planning must be. Choices you make affect all facets of your financial life.

R. Ratio or recipe (investments)

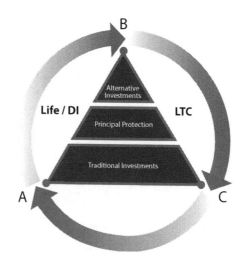

The next cornerstone of the comprehensive financial planning process is the R, representing a ratio or **recipe of differing assets** in your investment portfolio.

When you bake a cake, you use many ingredients: sugar, flour, milk, eggs, butter, salt. The trick to end up with a scrumptious cake is mixing those ingredients in the *right proportions*. You must add enough flour, enough sugar, not too many eggs, not too much salt, the right amount of milk—or else the cake will flop completely. In the same way, the right mix of asset classes in your investment portfolio can be "baked" into a wonderful return.

Look at the Investment Pyramid illustration above. Your accumulation and distribution life cycle revolves around this. The pyramid shows the three major classes of investment categories:

O Traditional,

O Principal Protected, and

O Alternative.

First, **traditional**. The traditional sector is the publicly traded markets. We talked about this exhaustively in Concept 2. Within the public markets the major categories include equities (stocks) and fixed income (bonds). Positions can be traded publicly, so value is readily available—creating transparency and liquidity. But this also creates potential for volatility.

Most firms and advisors solely focus on a "balanced portfolio" in traditional investments: stocks and bonds, mutual funds, exchange traded funds. Traditional investments are a great way to grow your asset base, because they typically have growth patterns. These growth patterns allow you to somewhat reliably accumulate wealth. You can buy and sell whenever you want, but this ready liquidity means that the market's short-term movement is volatile.

I believe a balanced portfolio is much more than the ratio of investments in equities and bonds in the traditional public markets. For this reason, I advise you to place only a certain percentage of your investment funds into publicly traded positions. Earlier in your accumulation phase, I recommend a greater percentage—but later, lacking the luxury of time to recover from bear markets, you will desire decreased volatility. Even bonds have become more volatile and less fixed in recent history, so dividing your assets between the publicly traded markets and other options needs to be carefully considered.

As a rule of thumb, you can place anywhere from 45% to 65% of your investment eggs into the traditional investments basket. Of course, within the traditional public market, I believe you should "own the entire market" through a diversified portfolio (as discussed in Concept 2).

The second category to add to your ingredients list is **principal protected** vehicles. If you put $100,000 into a principal protected vehicle, it will always be worth a minimum of $100,000. Such vehicles include CDs, money markets, and insurance contracts. These can all be written with guarantees and minimal (or zero) downside risk. Allocating some of your investable dollars into this category grants you stability, predictability, and security.

Remember the capped or indexed strategy we explored in Concept 2? Here is where the capped strategy coheres with your overall investment portfolio. Capped vehicles can be used to fulfill your need for principal protected vehicles.

A portfolio with principal protected vehicles is more than a simple diversified publicly traded portfolio. Combining traditional investments with principal protected vehicles adds layers of diversification, which translates to more predictable returns.

What is the disadvantage to principal protected assets? While they provide security, they are a long-term holding. Illiquidity is the main risk. When investing in this category of investment tools, you should put your money in and walk away for five or ten years. You might consider placing 20% to 35% of your investment eggs in principal protected assets.

The third asset class I recommend you add to your investment cake is alternative investments. My basic definition of an alternative investment is "any investment not traded on the public markets." Alternative investments are hard assets (such as real estate or oil and gas) or other commodities with associated income streams. These assets might lose value, but their value is based on tangible property. Tangible property may not be nearly as volatile as the traditional marketplace.

Why would you place some of your investment dollars into this asset class? Because it generally does not correlate with the publicly traded or principal protected classes. If the market drops into the abyss, alternative assets may not lose their value like the rest of your portfolio. Parts of your portfolio will zig, others will zag, but not all will diminish at the same time.

As with principal protected assets, alternative assets require a long-term investment horizon due to illiquidity. My recommendation ratio for alternatives is 5% to 10% of your investable assets.

Most advisors who call themselves "comprehensive planners" predominately push traditional market investments. They want to invest your money, and they want to manage it. As investment managers and fee-based advisors, they are not interested in the categories of principal protected or alternatives investments. This may be because they have little to no training in these areas. Or they may not be working wholeheartedly with you to achieve your financial life goals—they are pushing products rather than solutions. Not to mention, they might not be compensated financially for employing some of these very useful financial investment options within a true comprehensive plan. (More on fees and compensation later.)

Diversification improves when you layer principal protected vehicles and alternative non-publicly-traded vehicles with your traditional investments. Diversification does not guarantee against loss; it is a method used to manage risk. This helps you attain a more predictable return over time. What does this mean to you? Stability in your comprehensive portfolio and a greater chance to reach your financial goals.

E. Estate (estate and asset protection)

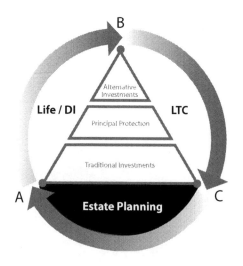

The fourth cornerstone of comprehensive financial planning is E, for estate planning and asset protection. Estate planning ensures the estate you have built up throughout your lifetime is left to your family and community as you desire. Attaining financial security and enjoying the life you want is sweet, but knowing your family is secure is sweeter still. Further, estate planning allows you to plan your life's lasting impact.

You can avail yourself of many tools to leave your desired legacy. Your lifetime of hard work can transcend into a meaningful endowment for the organizations you believe in. Sit down with your estate attorneys and set up your will, your durable power of attorney, your health care directive, and your revocable and irrevocable trusts. Always keep in mind how each applies to your unique situation and your goals. Also be sure to execute any further asset protection you need to make certain your wealth is appropriately distributed.

Summary: Finding the cure

As a doctor, you know you must have an established patient process in order to care for them and see them cured of their ailments. I had such a process when I practiced internal medicine: A patient would come in with a complaint. I would talk to them, compose a history, carry out a physical, order the lab tests, ask many questions, and ultimately diagnose. Upon reaching a diagnosis, you develop the treatment plan and prescribe medicines or delineate therapies.

But you do not simply leave it at that. You ask your patient to return after a certain amount of time so you can see if your plan of action is working. You check blood levels and evaluate the symptoms again. Maybe the condition has changed, or maybe there are unacceptable side effects. Maybe the patient does not respond to this course of action at all, so you have to go back to the drawing board and change the plan.

You have to modify, maintain, and monitor in order to return the patient to health. You pursue the problems until they are healed or managed appropriately. Because if you do not, your patient will suffer consequences—or die.

Effective financial planning is similar. You need to follow a process: establish needs and plan your approach so everything is addressed appropriately. Once matters have been implemented, you need to maintain and monitor and modify where necessary. Circumstances change and your needs and goals alter—expectedly or unexpectedly. You must reevaluate and make choices and changes.

What is your big picture? Do you really know? Sure, you know parts of it. But what about the parts you haven't considered?

Do you have the time and knowledge and access to tools necessary to create your comprehensive financial plan? If not, have you begun a long-term relationship with a planner who has access to the network of necessary professionals?

I believe working with a single trusted point of advocacy who understands your overall goals is the key to managing your financial planning. By stepping back and addressing each area as it relates to your big picture, you can maximize the benefits available in the complex world of financial planning.

Instead of spending your time managing a cadre of advisors, wouldn't it make sense to work with one professional who can coordinate all the pieces? Wouldn't it make sense to free up your time to and devote it to your personal and professional priorities? You want to pour yourself out—not into financial planning, but into your family and your patients.

The C.U.R.E. process addresses all these questions. This framework delivers truly comprehensive planning. It allows you to understand your plan in totality and locate any blind spots. It helps you prioritize your greatest needs. It aims at the completion of all aspects of your financial life plan. Please use this C.U.R.E. to ensure that you are on track.

Interlude.

What's Your Number?

To live a healthy life, you need to know your numbers. Two of the more important numbers are your weight and blood pressure. When you monitor these numbers you can make the necessary adjustments to live a full and prosperous life. Similarly, you should monitor certain numbers for the sake of your financial health.

After you comprehensively plan using the C.U.R.E. process, you want to regularly evaluate your position on the economic life cycle. Are the goals you are planning for still current? Monitor and adjust.

The reality is that saving money is hard. Saving enough money to retire is even harder. Only a fraction of the population ever achieves true financial independence. Consider the following graph:

As mentioned earlier, Point B on the Economic Life Cycle graph is the point at which you have accumulated sufficient resources to live. The money you earn from these assets supports your lifestyle. You no longer need to work to earn a living; your saved assets do the work for you.

What Is Your Number?

Yearly After Tax Retirement Income Goal

Age	$100,000	$200,000	$300,000
	Cash Needed at Age 65		
40	$3,615,099	$7,230,198	$10,845,297
45	3,118,416	6,236,832	9,355,248
50	2,689,973	5,379,946	8,069,919
55	2,320,394	4,640,788	6,961,182
60	2,001,593	4,003,186	6,004,779

Based upon 5% net rate of return on invested capital; 3% inflation; 20-year retirement period.

This is a hypothetical illustration of mathematical compounding and does not represent the performance of any specific investment product or class of investments. Rate of return will vary over time, particularly for long term investments. The values shown do not reflect product fees, charges or taxes which would reduce returns if included. Actual results will vary.

Suppose you were 45 years old and wanted to live on $100,000 per year from age 65 to age 85. How much money at age 65 would mean you had succeeded? The graph says you would need $3,118,416. Needless to say, saving over $3 million is difficult. But it does get slightly easier with a structured plan.

What if you wanted to live on $200,000 per year? If you were 55 years old now, you would need $4,640,788 saved by age 65. (These numbers do make some assumptions: 5% net rate of return on invested capital, 3% inflation, and 20 years of distributions.) You get the point. It is hard to accumulate enough funds to reach Point B.

As a financial planner for doctors I frequently encounter the following scenario: A young doctor exits the training phase and starts making more money than he ever has before. He decides he can retire in 15 years. Oh, the folly of youth…. Fast forward 15 years and he is in his 40s, married with three kids. Expenses galore! And the bank wants its mortgage payments. But he and his wife still believe they can retire before age 65. Fast forward another decade, and he is now in his 50s. He and his wife hope they can retire at age 65…all those lifestyle expenses and college tuition and wedding costs have taken their toll. Another decade later, the couple wonders if they will ever be able to retire. On the bright side, by this point many doctors love their work and do not want to retire yet.

Doctors' perspectives and goals change over time, as do the type and number of expenses. A big picture view frames the challenges, and following a coordinated financial plan can help you overcome these obstacles and reach your financial life goals.

How will you reach your savings goal? What is your goal, in the first place? When I speak to doctors they understand the idea of a *number*. They also assume they are being well taken care of. They usually have an advisor and (quite frankly) do not care to entertain yet another investment salesperson. But then I ask them, "What's your number?" Many doctors respond with a very quizzical face and ask me to clarify. Hopefully this chapter has clarified for you.

Again I ask you: How do you and your financial advocate answer the question, "What's your number?" If you do not know your number, how can you tell if you are on the path to achieving your short- and long-term goals? Maybe you have a salesperson and not a solution provider. You should strongly consider finding a real planning advocate to guide your financial future.

By monitoring your numbers, getting regular checkups, and staying healthy, you should be able to live worry-free. In your financial life, too, you absolutely can live free from the worry of ever running out of money.

Concept #5

Converting Assets to Income Inefficiently

The fifth and final financial planning concept doctors get wrong is figuring out how to take their hard earned assets and *convert those assets to income.*

Recall the doctors' economic life cycle from Concept 4?

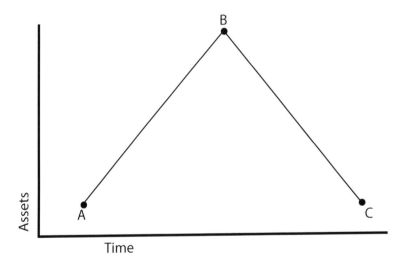

At Point A, you are finally earning more than you are losing to expenses. Now you have discretionary income to spend or invest. The rest of your working career up until retirement is the arc from Point A to Point B. At Point B, you are at last financially able to quit working. You have accumulated money and assets that you can live on, instead of having to generate new income.

Now you are on the arc between Point B and Point C. And questions begin to arise:

- How do you convert these funds into spendable income?
- How do you make sure your money lasts?
- How do you minimize the impact of taxes?

You need a plan. Do you have one?

The financial industry has done a good job of providing plenty of investment choices, ways to save and accumulate. But I believe the industry often fails to efficiently turn those assets into livable income. I see advisors selling and liquidating at their clients' requests, with nary a thought of whether the money will last—let alone a thought about tax efficiency.

In addition to the C.U.R.E. mixed investment pyramid, I have developed a five-step formula to create tax-efficient income for life. The formula guides you to account for everything retirement entails, both income and expenses. It will help you determine how to distribute funds in a tax-efficient manner. This consolidated distribution formulation helps ensure you do not lose more to taxes than you absolutely have to.

Math time

The first step in this five-step formula is to **determine what your expenses will be** during retirement. Be sure to distinguish between needs, wants, and wishes.

○ By *needs* I mean the basics: food, shelter, clothing, transportation. Absolute necessities.

○ *By wants and wishes* I mean discretionary items like travel, a new car, fine dining, expanding your antique furniture collection. Things you could live without.

By all means, list the retirement activities you have been planning your whole life. But think about the details. Do you plan to live at the same level or scale back a bit? Will you eat out more or fewer times each week? Do you want to live in town, or sell the house and stay at the lake all year round?

What does your dream retirement look like?

Do a little math and calculate your monthly expenses. Most doctors I talk to have no idea about their monthly expenses off the top of their heads. Figuring out how much you really spend can actually be a bit of work.

You intend here to determine your personal expenses, separate from your business expenses. During retirement you may no longer have connections to the business, so be thorough on the personal side. Pin down what your household will require per month to maintain the standard of living you desire during the next 30 years or so of retirement.

Envision your life in retirement and think about the expenses you will or might incur. Taking into account your lifestyle and goals, identify which expenses are essential, and differentiate them from those that are discretionary.

RETIREMENT INCOME NEED WORKSHEET

Monthly Expenses	Essential Amount	Discretionary Amount	Will It Vary? (Check If Yes)
Household Expenses			
Mortgage/Rent	$	$	☐
Utilities/Cable/Internet	$	$	☐
General Maintenance	$	$	☐
Household Supplies	$	$	☐
Property Tax & Insurance	$	$	☐
Credit Card Debt Payments	$	$	☐
Home Improvement	$	$	☐
New Purchases	$	$	☐
Household Exp. Subtotals	**$**	**$**	
Meals			
Groceries/ Beverages	$	$	☐
Entertaining/Dining Out	$	$	☐
Meals Subtotals	**$**	**$**	
Personal Care			
Clothing	$	$	☐
Products/Maintenance	$	$	☐
Personal Care Subtotals	**$**	**$**	
Healthcare			
Insurance Payments/Medicare	$	$	☐
Out-of-pocket Payments	$	$	☐
Dental/Optical	$	$	☐
Other Essential Expenses	$	$	☐
Healthcare Subtotals	**$**	**$**	

234 Office Park Drive Gulf Shores, AL 36542 · (251) 955-2827 · www.dykenwealthstrategies.com

RETIREMENT INCOME NEED WORKSHEET

Monthly Expenses	Essential Amount	Discretionary Amount	Will It Vary? (Check If Yes)
Transportation			
Car Payments/Auto Insurance	$	$	☐
Maintenance/Fuel	$	$	☐
Vacations	$	$	☐
Vehicle Upgrades	$	$	☐
Taxes, Registration, etc.	$	$	☐
Other Transportation Costs	$	$	☐
Transportation Subtotals	$	$	
Miscellaneous/Other			
Income Tax	$	$	☐
Gifts/Holidays	$	$	☐
Charitable Contributions	$	$	☐
Hobbies/Leisure	$	$	☐
	$	$	☐
	$	$	☐
Misc. Subtotals	$	$	

MONTHLY TOTALS

Total amounts for Essential & Discretionary Expenses $ $

X 12   X 12

ANNUAL TOTALS

Multiply by 12 to get the Total Annual Expenses $ $

↘   +   ↙

GRAND TOTAL

Add Annual Essential and Discretionary Expenses together to get the total Retirement Income Need. $

WEALTH STRATEGIES

One of the most important parts of retirement income planning is determining how much income you will need your portfolio to provide in retirement. This worksheet will help you calculate those numbers. By comparing your spending needs to your protected versus non-guaranteed income sources, you can determine the role your portfolio will play in providing income in retirement.

PROTECTED INCOME VS. PORTFOLIO INCOME

Protected Income Source	Owner	Description (Including Start & End Dates)	Annual Amount
Social Security			$
Social Security			$
Pension			$
Pension			$
Annuity Income			$
Annuity Income			$
Other			$
Other			$
		Protected Income Source Total:	$

Non-Guaranteed Income Source	Owner	Description (Including Start & End Dates)	Annual Amount
Part-time Work			$
Part-time Work			$
Rental Income			$
Gifts Received			$
Gifts Received			$
Other			$
Other			$
		Non-Guaranteed Income Source Total:	$

234 Office Park Drive Gulf Shores, AL 36542 · (251) 955-2827 · www.dykenwealthstrategies.com

	Annual Amount	
Protected Income Sources (from page 1)	$	
Non-Guaranteed Income Sources (from page 1)	$	
Income Total:	$	Box 1
Essential Expenses (from Retirement Income Need Worksheet)	$	
Discretionary Expenses (from Retirement Income Need Worksheet)	$	
Expenses Total:	$	Box 2
Subtract Expenses Total From Estimated Income (Box 1 - Box 2) :	$	Box 3

If the figure above is negative, it reflects the amount you will need from savings each year.

Retirement Savings Total (From Are Your Retirement Dollars Safe Worksheet):	$	Box 4

Now let's calculate your annual withdrawal percentage from your savings by dividing your needed income by your retirement savings.

Divide Box 3 by Box 4=	
Multiply by 100	X 100
Estimated Withdrawal Percentage from Retirement Savings	%

HOW DO TAXES IMPACT YOUR FUTURE LIFESTYLE INCOME?

Account Name:	Owner:	Tax Deferred (Qualified)	Taxable (Personal)	Tax Advantaged (Personal)	Unsure
Work Retirement Plan (401k, etc.)		$	$	$	$
Work Retirement Plan (401k, etc.)		$	$	$	$
Lump Sum Pension		$	$	$	$
Lump Sum Pension		$	$	$	$
IRA		$	$	$	$
IRA		$	$	$	$
Roth IRA		$	$	$	$
Roth IRA		$	$	$	$
Taxable Mutual Funds		$	$	$	$
Individual Bonds		$	$	$	$
Annuities		$	$	$	$
Annuities		$	$	$	$
Cash Savings (Checking, CDs, etc.)		$	$	$	$
Cash Savings (Checking, CDs, etc.)		$	$	$	$
Other:		$	$	$	$
Other:		$	$	$	$
Other:		$	$	$	$
Totals:		$	$	$	$

Totals:

Tax Deferred	Taxable	Tax Advantaged
$	$	$

Assumed Tax Rate ÷ 100:

Tax Due (Total X Tax Rate): $

Net Lifestyle Income:
(Total - Tax Due) $ $ $

Total Lifestyle Income: $
(Add all three Columns)

234 Office Park Drive Gulf Shores, AL 36542 · (251) 955-2827 · www.dykenwealthstrategies.com

The second step is to **identify your future sources of income.** Most doctors have a better idea of what their projected income sources will be than what their projected expenses will amount to. These sources include:

○ Social Security

○ A pension plan

○ Investments

○ IRA

○ Inheritance

○ And more

Just as there are two types of expenses, necessities (needs) and discretionary spending (wants and wishes), there are two types of income.

First is your *protected income.* These are dependable resources that are not subject to loss. Social Security belongs to this group. (Some would argue that Social Security is not a dependable source, because there may not be sufficient funds available for payment amounts promised. Regardless of your opinion on that, Social Security will at least not diminish due to a bear market. It provides a steady income every month.) Certain pension plans fall into protected income as well. Finally, certain types of income protected in the form of annuities or loans from principal protected insurance sources also fit in the protected category.

Then you have *variable income* sources. They are "variable" because their value is based on distribution rates, taxes, market volatility, illiquidity, and other variable factors. These sources are less dependable: The market may have a correction. You may have value in a piece of real estate that you cannot sell. In truth, there is a lot to worry about with these future sources of income.

So now you have your income broken down into two categories: protected sources and volatile sources. Previously, you listed your two types of future expenses: needs and wants/wishes. Why did we break down the two types of income and the two types of expenses? To try to match these two and provide you some security in your retirement life. We want to measure the security of your lifestyle, then balance it with the retirement dream opportunities time and money can give provide you.

The third step in our income planning formula is **matching the different types of income streams to the different types of expenses.** By this I mean matching up your non-negotiable necessities with stable income sources, and matching up your discretionary expenses with variable income sources. This way your basic needs will always be provided for, even if your discretionary money varies. You may have less to spend on play and travel and new cars than you hoped, but at least you have no worries about food and clothing and shelter.

The fear of outliving their money plagues retirees. This planning formula eliminates that fear. You can see on paper that your monthly Social Security check and other protected income sources will cover your food and medicine and utilities. Sure, you may have to drive the Buick a few more thousand miles—but your basic needs are covered.

The investment you have earmarked for a new car is volatile. You may not be able to buy immediately. But if you are patient and do not panic, then over time you should have the funds to buy a Buick. Or perhaps something even better! That is the positive side of variable income sources. They can grow substantially more than your safe investments, opening up vistas of opportunity.

Your stable income sources confirm that the expenses necessary for existence will always be covered, from groceries to mortgages. On top of that, you can adapt your plan based on future events without jeopardizing your security.

I do not see the average advisor engaging in this level of planning. Many of them do not even seem to understand how to carry out real retirement income planning. Expenses are all the same to them, and assets are just assets to be utilized. They do not have detailed conversations. But these conversations form the basis of their clients' peace and confidence.

Now we arrive at the fourth part of this formula. After you have matched your income and expenses, check that your plan takes advantage of your asset structure in **minimizing taxation.**

Recall when we looked at the three tax buckets in Concept 1?

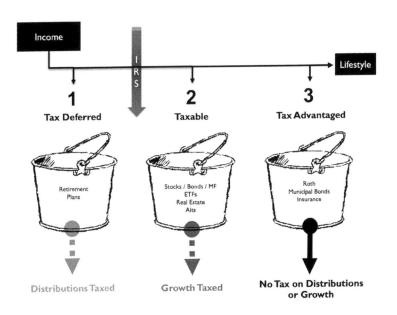

Each of these buckets has a distribution tax consequence:

○ When you want to take money out of the Tax Deferred Bucket, there will be income tax.

○ When you liquidate positions in the Taxable Bucket, there will be capital gains taxes.

○ When you take money out of the Tax Advantaged Bucket, no tax occurs.

If you have assets in each bucket, you can work to reduce your taxable income. Strategizing the combination and timing of distributions from these three buckets helps create a blended, minimized tax.

If you need $200,000 per year and you take it all from the tax-deferred bucket, you're going to pay tax on $200,000. If you take only $100,000 from the tax-deferred bucket and the other $100,000 from the tax-advantaged bucket, you pay taxes only on the $100,000. Picking which tax bucket to take money out of is as important as which asset class within the bucket you draw from. Some moves are more tax-savvy than others.

Another way of phrasing the fourth part of this strategy is to *prioritize and time your asset distributions* to minimize your tax burden and give you lifestyle liberties. Fewer taxes means more money for you—not for the government.

Finally, step five is to **maintain and monitor.** Current projections estimate that the average couple will be in retirement for close to 30 years. *You have to plan and predict income streams for 30 years.* You and I know that matters do not stay stable over 30-year time frames. You will modify: maybe scale back expenses, increase income, manage taxation. Or maybe you will scale up a bit, after you receive an inheritance or after one of your investment performs phenomenally. Also, how will things change if your spouse passes away? This is a dynamic, living, breathing plan—not a static equation on a page in a drawer. You should check in regularly. If your goals or needs or situation changes, you will make the appropriate course correction.

If you are still a number of years away from retirement, you do not have to sit down and set these numbers in concrete. You can keep the ideas in the back of your head for now and focus on accumulation. However, planning ahead once you get closer to retirement will contribute toward alleviating your concerns and stress level. Staying acquainted with these steps and formulas, you can manage risk deliberately and feel confident in your investments across the board. When you step into retirement, you will know where your money is coming from.

This five-step formula can be used to start planning the next phase of your life. Your golden years can be secure and enjoyable. The conversion of your assets to spendable dollars should be looked forward to, not dreaded. With proper financial life planning, you can achieve all your financial life goals. This is Comprehensive Planning.

A Word About Fees

"Paying the piper" is an idiom that refers to accepting the consequences of our actions. This holds true in life, health, and finances. Many doctors are paying a high price for decisions about their retirement savings they made years ago. Thankfully, most of the time we can help them recover and restore them to their desired financial position.

During these conversations one topic routinely comes up. What should you pay for comprehensive planning? (Assuming you have found a real comprehensive planner, and not an imposter.) This is an important question. A wide variety of compensation models exist: some less expensive, some more so. You should consider the fees—but you should also consider the value you receive.

There is no single standard for fees. As discussed previously, a wide range of services and products are involved in delivering comprehensive financial planning. Thus, the compensation varies also.

Traditionally, the financial services industry used a commission -based compensation model. Products you purchased generated a commission for the advisor or agent. This fee was typically determined by the product type and product provider. The advisor acted as an agent brokering the deal.

As the financial industry evolved, the fee-based model came into being. In this model, you pay a percentage of your assets under management to the agent of record. That creates revenue for the advisor, based on the total magnitude of investable assets.

As the assets increase in value, fees increase. If assets diminish, advisor compensation does too.

Many marketing dollars are spent trying to suggest that one fee model is better than the other. Many fee-only advisors promote themselves as using a better compensation model than the traditional commissioned structure. I do believe that the fee-based model better aligns your goals and the advisor's compensation. However, not all commissioned products are bad. In fact, some products can only be accessed via a commissioned platform. Exclusively fee-based advisors may be forced to exclude important components of your planning—particularly those related to principal protected and alternative investments.

Additionally, some elements of a truly comprehensive financial plan are unrelated to investment assets. These include:

- debt reduction strategies,
- structuring business and personal entities,
- insurance services,
- asset protection, and
- estate planning.

These services are extremely necessary. If your planner focuses solely on assets under management, however, such issues may take a back seat. Do not ignore this aspect of planning.

You should be able to locate a planner who will charge a one-time setup fee for these services, or an annual fee to design, implement, monitor, and maintain. I believe money spent on this planning is a proactive way to create long-term value.

Be wary of making financial decisions solely due to fees. Shopping for the cheapest alternative is prudent—but do not miss the value a real planner provides. As in the healthcare industry, you get what you pay for. Saving pennies on the front end may cost you dollars down the road. Decide because of value and price.

One variable is your level of involvement. Some doctors I work with require very little assistance, as they enjoy investing themselves. Others tell me financial planning is the last thing they want to do—just take care of it! Because of this variable, the level of planning, investment, and other services you need is uniquely personal. Likewise, the fee schedule varies depending on the desired level and expanse of planning.

Be wary of conflicts of interest. Ask for as much transparency as possible on the fees you will pay for services rendered. But know that all services do have a cost, and you do not want an advisor to offer you low prices because he is skimping on staff and resources. Poor planners can be just as dangerous as poor doctors. Be informed. Be conscious of what type of financial planning support you need, as well as the appropriate price.

Acknowledgements

I would like to thank the experts at Paperback Experts for their clear process and never ending guidance that without their help this book would not have happened. Specifically, Michael and Caleb DeLon for their understanding and expertise in bringing this book to fruition.

Additionally, I would like to thank the incredible partners I have at Dyken Wealth Strategies including Michelle Stancil and Colleen Fay. They helped and supported every aspect of this publication. Their perspective helped to make our story clearer.

Over the 25 years of working with healthcare professional I have had amazing mentors and colleagues that have helped shape my perspective and thoughts on financial matters and their impact on healthcare. Special credit goes to Dr. Donald Guess who shaped my early thoughts on planning and gave me the opportunity to enter into this wonderful field of planning that gives me such joy. Many fellow advisors have mentored me and shared their expertise over the years including Rob Cheney, Ed Siddell, Ryan Peterson, Shane Hunt, and too many others to list here. My gratitude goes out to each and every one of them.

To my family, my wife Renee, my four incredible children; Jace, Landon, Colton, and Carmon I thank you for your unconditional love and support that fills my life with joy.

All these blessings come from the love and grace of God through whom all things are possible.

About Jason

Dr. Jason Dyken attended Furman University and graduated *magna cum laude* with a bachelor's degree in chemistry. He attended medical school at the University of South Alabama, graduating in 1991. After his residency in internal medicine, Dr. Dyken practiced in multiple healthcare settings: academic medicine, private practice, and employed physician. While practicing, he recognized the changing business climate in medicine and decided to attend graduate school. Dr. Dyken received his M.B.A. from the University of Alabama at Birmingham with honors, still practicing medicine full time.

After a decade of practice, Jason realized he could impact doctors through wealth planning rather than as a practitioner and hospital Chief of Staff. He became licensed as a wealth strategist and began taking on doctors as clients. In 2001, he retired from full-time medical practice and started Dyken Wealth Strategies.

Jason has since dedicated his professional career to meeting the financial planning needs of doctors and their families. He works with physicians and dentists to define, simplify, and execute strategies intended to protect their financial future. Jason passionately desires to long-term trusted relationships on which financial confidence can be built. His structured approach to wealthcare development considers individual vision and need, then fashions customized solutions to support each personal and financial legacy.

Jason's passion for his clients extends to his community. He is currently serving his third term as city councilman for the City of Gulf Shores, and was appointed as the chairman of the Finance Committee. Jason also serves on the Airport Authority for the

Jack Edwards National Airport, as well as the Gulf Coast Health-care Authority. He has represented the banking and finance sector for the Coastal Resiliency Coalition, an organization instrumental in communities' recovery from the 2010 Deepwater Horizon oil spill. Jason is committed to education: he is a patron of the Gulf Shores Elementary School, and has been intimately involved in designing and promoting educational excellence. He and his family are members of the Gulf Shores United Methodist Church.

Jason and his wife of over 23 years, Dr. Renee Dyken (an orthodontist practicing in Gulf Shores and Mobile), have four children: Jason, Landon, Colton, and Carmon. He enjoys physical activity, water sports, and spending time with his family and friends.

About Dyken Wealth Strategies

The mission of Dyken Wealth Strategies is to improve doctors' lives by helping them make good financial decisions. Our logo says it all.

Dyken

It is natural to assume I named Dyken Wealth Strategies after myself. Actually, I wanted to use the Dyken name to honor my father and his brother. They were raised in very challenging times, yet succeeded through hard work, integrity, honesty, and commitment to act uprightly. My father and uncle attended medical school and choose the honorable profession of medicine for their lives' work. Rather than enter lucrative private practice, both became academic physicians and rose to national leadership in their fields of specialty. They always focused on promoting education and the doctor-patient relationship. Their careers embodied the essence of why every good doctor enters the industry: to provide care, comfort, and understanding to patients in need.

Healthcare has become complicated. Many of us have lost the *why* for our career. I hope that proper financial life planning will instill economic confidence in you, enabling you to return to the essence of healthcare. Because of this, I wanted to honor my relatives' name and careers. I wanted to honor the integrity of the healthcare profession and remember why I practice wealthcare. My desire is to help doctors become financially independent, take care of their families, provide better care for their patients, and improve their society and community. As a trusted financial advocate, I pledge to doctors the same amount of dedication they pledge to their patients.

You do not have to worry about the business and economics of healthcare. Proper planning can eliminate them—achieving financial security for your family grants freedom. That is my first wealthcare goal.

Once you have taken care of your family, another opportunity will arise. Doctors are the best and brightest our society has to offer. Additionally, doctors are caring and giving individuals. With proper planning, a doctor and family will have more financial resources than they wish to use. These resources can be leveraged to create legacies that will improve our communities and society for all. Endowing a doctor's value system through proper planning can leave a legacy of a life well lived.

Wealth Strategies

Wealth strategies are our specialty. Our approach is comprehensive financial life planning, focusing on all a doctor's needs. Individualization adds a personal element that strategically positions the doctor for financial success. We help doctors secure financial freedom for their families and establish a legacy of their life's work.

Investment Diversification

The pyramid within the capital D schematically represents our implementation strategy. Clients of Dyken Wealth Strategies benefit from the C.U.R.E. process, our unique approach that addresses the four cornerstones of planning.

Rod of Asclepius

The Rod of Asclepius continues to be the dominant symbol for professional healthcare associations in the United States. The single serpent-entwined rod was wielded by the Greek god Asclepius, a deity associated with healing and medicine. The original Hippocratic Oath began with the invocation, "I swear by Apollo the Physician and by Asclepius and by Hygieia...."

As a doctor-owned and -operated financial planning firm focusing exclusively on doctors, Dyken Wealth Strategies is committed to the healthcare profession. Sharing the common symbol of the Rod of Asclepius, we apply the same principles of integrity and honor to the financial services industry as the Rod of Asclepius does for healthcare.

Made in the USA
Middletown, DE
24 January 2017